DAYS THAT SHOOK THE WORLD
NOVEMBER 9, 1989

THE FALL OF THE BERLIN WALL

DAYS THAT SHOOK THE WORLD

The Fall of the Berlin Wall

NOVEMBER 9, 1989

Pat Levy

RAINTREE
STECK·VAUGHN
RSVP® PUBLISHERS

A Harcourt Company

Austin   New York
www.raintreesteckvaughn.com

DAYS THAT SHOOK THE WORLD

Assassination in Sarajevo   Hiroshima
The Chernobyl Disaster   The Kennedy Assassination
D-Day   The Moon Landing
The Dream of Martin Luther King   Pearl Harbor
The Fall of the Berlin Wall   The Wall Street Crash

Published by Raintree Steck-Vaughn Publishers,
an imprint of Steck-Vaughn Company

Library of Congress Cataloging-in-Publication Data is available upon request.

ISBN 0-7398-5233-7

Printed in Italy. Bound in the United States.

1 2 3 4 5 6 7 8 9 0 LB 06 05 04 03 02

Picture Acknowledgments:

Cover picture: Celebrations on the Berlin Wall on
November 9, 1989 (Camera Press/ERMA).
Title page picture: East German guards prepare to defend the Brandenburg Gate as celebrating West Germans gather on November 10, 1989 (AKG London/F Gaul).

We are grateful to the following for permission to reproduce photographs:
AKG London 9, 10, 11 bottom, 15 (East German Press), 19 bottom, 21, 23 top, 26, 27 (F. Gaul), 36 (Dieter E. Hoppe), 37 bottom (Dieter E Hoppe), 46; Associated Press 16 left (Kreusch), 20, 43 top (Jan Bauer), 43 bottom (Thomas Kienzle); Camera Press 14, 18, 23 bottom (ERMA), 24 (ERMA), 29 top (ERMA), 30 (ERMA), 40 (Sven Simon); Corbis 32 (Robert Maass), 37 top (Gregor Schmid), 38 (Robert Maass); Corbis/Bettmann Archive 8, 11 top, 12, 13, 19 top; Popperfoto/Reuters 22, 25 right, 29 bottom, 34, 35 top, 42; Topham Picturepoint 6, 7, 16 right, 17, 25 (AP), 28 (AP), 31 (AP), 33 (AP), 35 bottom (AP), 41; UNHCR 39 (LeMoyne). Artwork by Michael Posen.

CONTENTS

East German soldiers stand guard on top of the Berlin Wall, built to prevent East Berliners from escaping to West Berlin.

ON THE AFTERNOON OF November 9, 1989, a meeting of the East German government was taking place in East Berlin. No one present realized that this meeting would have extraordinary consequences. It would, in fact, lead to a moment that changed world history—the fall of the Berlin Wall.

By 1989, Germany had been a divided country for over 40 years. West Germany and East Germany were two separate countries, each with its own government and its own capital city. The borders between the two countries were closed. Berlin, deep inside East Germany, was also a divided city. A concrete barrier, the Berlin Wall, ran through it. Those living on the eastern side of the wall were citizens of East Germany. Those living on the other side of the wall were citizens of West Germany, even though their city lay within East Germany. The wall had been built to prevent East Germans from crossing from East to West Berlin.

Now East Germany was facing a crisis. Its government, like most of those in Eastern Europe, had been under the control of the communist Soviet Union for decades. But the Soviet Union was going through a period of reform under its leader Mikhail Gorbachev. For several years, Gorbachev had been relaxing the strict laws by which communist governments ruled. East European countries had begun to make similar reforms. One of them, Hungary, now had a more liberal government—which had decided to open its borders to the West. For the first time in many years, people were being allowed to leave Hungary and travel into Western Europe. East Germans had begun leaving their country in large numbers—pouring through Czechoslovakia into Hungary, and then crossing the border into Austria.

At the meeting on November 9, the leader of the East German government, Egon Krenz, tried to deal with the crisis. He announced that a new law would allow citizens to travel or emigrate to the West, but only after they had applied for a passport and a visa. It was thought that forcing people to make this application would slow down the rate at which they were leaving.

Gunter Schabowski, a high-ranking politician, turned up late for the meeting. His copy of the new law was pushed over the table to him, and he was told to make it public. That evening, Schabowski met journalists in East Berlin for a press conference. He was to outline recent changes in the work of the government. Schabowski pulled out his latest piece of paper, scanned its contents for the first time and read it aloud. Without realizing it, he made an announcement that prepared the way for the fall of the Berlin Wall—and for the reunification of Germany.

A Moment in Time

At 6:00 P.M. on November 9,1989, in a stuffy East Berlin hall, a press conference is taking place. Gunter Schabowski, the government spokesman, makes a closing statement: "Today, the decision was taken to make it possible for all citizens to leave the country through the official border crossing points. All citizens can now be issued with visas for the purpose of travel or visiting relatives in the West. The order is to take effect at once...." Journalists shout: "When? How soon?" Schabowski scans his note, then replies: "It just means right away." The room empties.

An East German celebrates on September 11, 1989, as he crosses the Hungarian border into Austria and the freedom of the West.

Soldiers from the Soviet Union hoist their country's flag over the Brandenburg Gate in Berlin, to celebrate victory over Germany in World War II.

A Divided Family

" The main house was in the Soviet zone, while some of the fields were in the British zone. The border literally divided the property. Aged 17, my father hid a suitcase on a horse-drawn cart and drove west across the border on family property, leaving his parents behind. In the following 40 years he was allowed to return only twice—for a maximum of three hours each time—for their funerals. "

Author Oliver August, in Along the Wall and Watchtowers, *remembers how the partitioning of Germany divided the farmland where his father was growing up.*

WORLD WAR II came to an end in Europe in May 1945, with victory for the Allies—led by the United States, the Soviet Union, and Great Britain—over Nazi Germany. Long before this, the Allies had considered the problem of how to deal with a defeated Germany. At first, as a way of making sure that Germany could never again become too powerful, they had proposed breaking up the country into a number of smaller states, each with its own government. But this idea had been replaced by a plan to partition, or divide up, Germany among the United States, the Soviet Union, Great Britain, and France. This was to be a temporary partitioning, with each of the Allies in military control of its own zone, until a new and trusted administration could once again govern a united Germany. At a conference in London in 1944, the borders of these zones had been agreed upon.

It was logical for the Soviet Union to be given control of the eastern part of Germany. The Soviet army had advanced from the east, pushing back the German army that had invaded and tried to conquer the Soviet

GREAT BRITAIN · NETHERLANDS · London · Amsterdam · BRITISH ZONE · Air corridors · POLAND · Berlin · Warsaw · GERMANY · SOVIET ZONE · Brussels · Bonn · BELGIUM · Paris · FRENCH ZONE · U.S. ZONE · Prague · CZECHOSLOVAKIA · LUXEMBOURG · Vienna · FRANCE · Bern · SWITZERLAND · AUSTRIA · HUNGARY · Budapest · ROMANIA · Bucharest · Belgrade · MEDITERRANEAN SEA · ITALY · YUGOSLAVIA · BULGARIA · Sofia · Rome · ALBANIA · Tirana · GREECE · TURKEY · Athens · Moscow · SOVIET UNION · BLACK SEA

Km 0 300 600
Miles 0 200 400

EUROPE IN 1945

Germany and Berlin were partitioned among France, Great Britain, the U.S., and the Soviet Union.

Km 0 5 10 15
Miles 0 5 10

FRENCH SECTOR · Tegel · SOVIET SECTOR · BRITISH SECTOR · Gatow · Tempelhof · U.S. SECTOR

BERLIN DIVIDED

Union. In two world wars, the Soviets had seen their country invaded from the west. Now they wanted to ensure their future security by making countries such as Poland and Czechoslovakia (today divided into the Czech Republic and Slovakia) into "buffer states" on their western border.

The American, British, and French zones would be situated in the western half of Germany. A decision had also been made in London in 1944 about Berlin, the German capital, which was located in what would become the Soviet zone. It had been agreed that the city should also be divided into four sectors, with each of the Allies controlling a sector with its military force.

Berlin, like most German cities, was in ruins by the end of World War II. Its people were starving. As the summer of 1945 turned into winter, and the Allied forces settled into their sectors of occupation, arguments developed over how supplies should be moved around the city. More important, a political struggle between the Soviet Union and the United States began, as each tried to gain influence over the divided and shattered country of Germany. This struggle would turn into what became known as the Cold War.

As the United States and the Soviet Union developed into the two great superpowers of the world, the city of Berlin would become a world stage for the conflict between them.

In the summer of 1945, Berlin's starving citizens receive potatoes from the occupying forces.

9

THE PARTITION OF GERMANY would last for over 40 years, largely because of the development of the Cold War. This conflict set the powers of the West—led by the United States, Great Britain, and France—in opposition to the Eastern Bloc—the Soviet Union and the other communist countries of Eastern Europe. The two sides had opposing views about how their countries' economic and social systems should be organized. The Cold War never developed into open and armed war between the two superpowers, but it sometimes came very close to doing so.

Each side in the Cold War wanted to ensure that the part of Germany it controlled would develop according to its own plans. For the Soviet Union this meant communism, which required authoritarian rule and an economic system controlled by central government. For the United States it meant democracy and capitalism, an economic system based upon competition for profit among private companies.

In 1948, a new currency called the Deutsche mark was introduced into the American, British, and French zones of Germany, but not the Soviet zone. This made it clear that the two sides would not agree on an economic system common to all of Germany. When the new currency was extended to the western half of Berlin, the Soviet leaders responded angrily by blockading that half of the city. Over two million people in the west of Berlin relied on 12,000 tons of supplies brought in daily along the one road and one rail route that the Soviet Union allowed through its zone of Germany. In June 1948, the Soviet Union closed these routes and cut off the electricity supply. In a month, the people in the west of Berlin would begin to starve.

A West Berlin policeman checks cars leaving East Berlin in February 1949. The division of the city into two halves had already begun.

An American plane flies into West Berlin in May 1949, carrying much-needed supplies.

A little girl in West Berlin in June 1949, celebrating the arrival of fresh milk after the lifting of the blockade.

Germany, with Bonn as its capital. Five months later, the eastern part of Germany and the eastern part of Berlin became the German Democratic Republic. This was known as East Germany, and the eastern part of Berlin became its capital. The country of Germany was now divided into two separate states, and divided Berlin had two names: West Berlin and East Berlin. The beginnings of the Cold War had redrawn the map of central Europe.

The leaders of the western powers came to the city's rescue by mounting a massive airlift. Many different aircraft, including ramshackle old bombers, carried supplies into the city. By the spring of 1949, 8,000 tons of food and other supplies were being airlifted into Berlin every day. In May, the Soviet Union accepted defeat and lifted the blockade.

Also in May, the western part of Germany and the western part of Berlin were named the Federal Republic of Germany. This became known as West

An Iron Curtain

Winston Churchill, Great Britain's prime minister during World War II, made a speech in 1946 in Fulton, Missouri. He drew attention to the way postwar Europe was dividing into two opposing groups of countries, and said: "From Stettin in the Baltic to Trieste on the Adriatic an iron curtain has descended over the continent." By the end of the Berlin blockade, this was indeed seen to be the case. In time, this iron curtain would take on a very physical form, in the shape of the Berlin Wall.

On October 16, 1961, an American soldier faces an East German officer across the white line that divided Berlin.

A White Line

Between 1949 and 1961, Berlin was a divided city but there was no wall separating its two halves. Indeed, in some places in 1949 there was only a white line painted on the road to show where the border was. Buses and trains ran freely across the whole city, and so did telephone lines. Depending on the side of the city in which citizens lived, they were required to pay for train tickets and settle such things as telephone bills in either East German or *West German* currency.

EVEN AFTER EAST GERMANY and West Germany closed their border in 1952, people could move freely across the whole of Berlin. But the political divisions of the Cold War were already clear in the city. Each side of Berlin had its own police force. Each side also had its own army. The people of West Berlin lived in a city surrounded by the East German state, and to reach West Germany they had to travel more than 100 miles (160 km) by one of three ways: air, train, or road. There was only one railroad line and one road, with no garages or rest facilities between West Berlin and the West German border. Commercial flights into West Berlin could only be provided by American, British, and French airlines. These airlines could only fly through East Germany along three air routes, or "corridors." These corridors had been agreed upon by the four wartime allies in 1946, and had been used to airlift supplies during the Berlin blockade.

Although West Berlin was physically isolated inside East Germany, West Berliners did not live the kind of restricted life that many people imagined. In fact, the effect of the Cold War resulted in some advantages for West Berliners. Western powers wanted to make their part of Berlin a showcase for capitalism and democracy. American money was used to help rebuild West Berlin, and West German companies were encouraged to set up their factories there.

East Berlin developed in a different way. Under the communist system of East Germany, East Berlin provided its citizens with guaranteed employment, low rents, and free medical care. But there were also disadvantages. There was not the same level of wealth. The economy was not supported as generously as in West Berlin, and the city began to fall into disrepair. In June 1953, the poor conditions in East Berlin led to an

uprising: Thousands of workers went on strike to protest their working conditions. The strikes ended only after troops from the Soviet Union were sent in to restore order.

Berlin remained at the center of the continuing Cold War. Politicians from both sides talked about reuniting Germany. But Berlin not only remained divided, it became a symbol of the differences between the two superpowers. In 1958, Nikita Khrushchev, the Soviet leader, criticized the United States for placing nuclear weapons in West Germany. He also called for the whole of Berlin to become the capital of East Germany. In contrast, the American president, John F. Kennedy, spoke in July 1961 of West Berlin as "the great testing place of Western courage and will."

West Berlin police take an East Berlin citizen into protective custody after he crossed the border during the riots of 1953.

East German soldiers oversee the creation of a permanent concrete wall between East and West Berlin.

Erich Honecker (1912–1994)

The building of the Berlin Wall was masterminded by the hard-line communist Erich Honecker. He was responsible for military and security affairs in East Germany from 1958 until 1971. A member of the Communist Party since 1929, Honecker was elected to the politburo in 1958. He became leader of East Germany in 1971, and ruled the country until 1989, when he was forced to resign. In 1992, he was tried for manslaughter for ordering guards to shoot people trying to escape over the Berlin Wall. His ill-health prevented the trial's completion, and Honecker was instead exiled to Chile.

IN THE EARLY HOURS of Sunday, August 13, 1961, mobile lamps illumined East German police, firefighters, and customs officials as they unfurled huge rolls of barbed wire in the streets of Berlin. Armed soldiers formed a line along the border, standing with their backs to West Berlin. Civilians watched, amazed, as armed vehicles, trucks, and heavy machinery drew up. The East Germans now began building what would become known as the Berlin Wall. This barrier would eventually surround the whole of West Berlin.

The East German government's motive for building the Berlin Wall was an urgent need to stop large numbers of East Germans from leaving their country. The border between East and West Germany had been closed since 1952, but there was nothing to prevent East Germans from traveling to East Berlin and crossing over freely to West Berlin. They could then choose either to live there or be flown out to West Germany. Between 1949 and 1961, around 15 percent of East Germany's population of 17 million people made their way to West Germany.

During the first half of 1961, the number of East Germans leaving through Berlin had reached alarming proportions. Nearly 20,000 had left in March alone. Many of these were skilled workers and professionals, and as a result the East German economy was in serious danger of collapse. The higher standard of living in West Germany was an attraction for many East Germans. They were also worried by the buildup of American and Soviet troops in the two halves of Germany. The Cold War was heating up, and people feared that the borders might soon be closed.

Berliners awoke on August 12, 1961, to the dramatic news. On the radio and across telephone lines, word spread that the barrier being built through the city was no temporary measure. The entire 27-mile (43-km) boundary between East and West Berlin was being closed, permanently. At 6:00 P.M., West Berliners gathered on their side of the Brandenburg Gate, a famous landmark just inside East Berlin. They carried placards saying: "There is only one Germany." With growing anger, the crowd surged forward, chanting and hurling stones across the wire. East German soldiers armed with machine guns confronted the protesters. Some soldiers, realizing how close their colleagues were to opening fire, yelled across to West German police to hold back the crowds. The East German soldiers then used water-cannon to disperse the protesters. They defused a situation that could easily have become a bloodbath.

In the coming weeks, the barbed wire barrier across Berlin would be transformed into a concrete wall. It would be 28 years before this wall was removed.

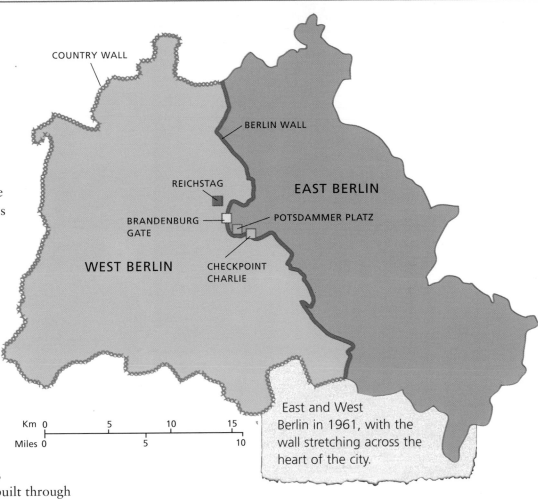

East and West Berlin in 1961, with the wall stretching across the heart of the city.

On August 12, 1961, East German soldiers guarded the Brandenburg Gate as West Berliners protested against the building of the wall.

On October 28, 1961, American tanks (foreground) and Soviet tanks confront each other at Checkpoint Charlie. The crisis came about after American diplomats were denied access to East Berlin.

IN THE DAYS FOLLOWING August 13, 1961, as the barbed wire began to be replaced by blocks of concrete, it became clear that the United States and its western allies would not confront the Soviet Union over the building of the Berlin Wall. Demonstrators on the western side of the wall marched with placards that read: "Betrayed by the West." But the U.S. president, John F. Kennedy, was forced to accept the situation because, as he wrote, "only war could reverse it."

In October 1961, it seemed that war might come. East German guards denied some American diplomats access to East Berlin. The small disagreement grew out of control, to the point where Soviet and American tanks were facing each other at a crossing point known as "Checkpoint Charlie." It was one of the most perilous moments in the Cold War. But Kennedy and Khrushchev, the leaders of the two superpowers, pulled back from armed confrontation.

An elderly woman prepares to jump to the freedom of the West from her fourth-floor apartment.

At first, some East Berliners found ways to cross the divided city. The border splitting the city followed traditional divisions between the old districts of Berlin, and the wall was formed in places by the walls of houses. Some people's homes stood in East Berlin, while their front doors opened into West Berlin. East German guards boarded up these doors, only for whole families to escape through windows using ropes of knotted bed sheets.

Between 1961 and 1989, about 5,000 people escaped from East to West Berlin. Balloons and pedal-power airplanes were used more than once, tunnels were dug, and people were smuggled across the border inside industrial machinery. One of the more amazing escapes was arranged by a circus manager. He managed to smuggle acrobats across the border one by one in a trunk. Another extraordinary escape involved a man whose wife had not been allowed to join him in West Berlin. He made a day trip to East Berlin with a woman who resembled his wife, stole her identity papers, and then used them to return with his real wife. The unfortunate other woman spent two years in jail in East Berlin, and the man was sentenced to seven months imprisonment by a West German court.

Many people lost their lives in their attempts to cross the Berlin Wall. In June 1962, an East German border guard was shot and killed by a man escaping. Two months later, a young man named Peter Fechter was shot by East German guards while attempting to escape, and was left to bleed to death within sight of American troops. He was the first of 192 people who would die trying to escape across the Berlin Wall. Their deaths were regular reminders of the grim reality of the wall, and the deadly nature of the Cold War.

The Wall 1961–1989

Total border length surrounding West Berlin	96 mi (155 km)
Border between East and West Berlin	27 mi (43 km)
Concrete wall	12 ft (3.6 m) high, 66 mi (106 km) long
Wire-mesh fencing	41 mi (66 km)
Anti-vehicle trenches	65 mi (105 km)
Number of watchtowers	302
Number of bunkers	20
Persons succeeded in crossing the wall	c. 5,000
Persons arrested in the border area	c. 3,200
Persons killed on the wall	192
Persons injured by shooting	c. 200

The body of Peter Fechter, the first person to be killed attempting to cross the wall, is recovered by East German guards.

With the wall dividing families, people stood on ladders to wave to their relatives across the barrier.

I N THE YEARS FOLLOWING the building of the wall, Berliners got on with the task of living under its shadow. The West German government encouraged its citizens to live in West Berlin by lowering rates of income tax compared to the rest of the country. Housing was also subsidized in West Berlin, and young people living there were not required to do military service—which was compulsory in the rest of West Germany. The government pumped money into West Berlin, and subsidized hotel rates were used to encourage people to visit the city. As tourists flocked into West Berlin, the Berlin Wall found itself in a new role—as a tourist attraction.

For East Berliners, life also began to improve. They enjoyed excellent health care, day-care facilities, virtually free public transportation, full employment, and subsidized food and rents. With skilled workers no longer deserting to the West, output from factories rose dramatically in the 1960s. Many East Germans genuinely believed that their communist system was fairer than the capitalism of West Berlin, and they grew proud of their achievements.

But East Berliners lacked some of the key freedoms enjoyed by West Berliners. They didn't have freedom of speech, free elections, or the right to leave their country and travel freely to the West.

While Berliners were settling into life with the wall, Soviet attitudes toward the rest of Eastern Europe were hardening. The building of the wall was not the only sign that force was necessary to impose the Soviet system of government. In 1956, 3,000 people had been killed when Soviet troops were sent to put down a revolt against the communist regime in Hungary. In 1968, reforms took place in Czechoslovakia, in what became known as the "Prague Spring." The leader of the government, Alexander Dubçek, tried to introduce what he called "communism with a human face." But his moves toward democracy were ended abruptly in August 1968, when Soviet tanks rumbled into Prague.

In Prague, in August 1968, crowds surround the Soviet troops brought in to suppress the reforms known as the "Prague Spring."

In the 1970s, it was Poland's turn to campaign for more freedoms. The people's calls for reform were led by the trade union movement known as Solidarity. But this movement was also put down with force, this time by Poland's own troops. It was clear that the Soviet Union and the communist governments of the Eastern Bloc were not yet ready to tear down walls of any kind.

A Moment in Time

On June 26, 1963, President John F. Kennedy, during a visit to express American support for West Berlin, stands on the balcony of the city's town hall. He looks out over a quarter of a million West Berliners, and beyond them to the wall. It has become a symbol of the divisions of the Cold War. To cheers from the crowd, Kennedy makes a famous speech that ends: "All free men, wherever they may live, are citizens of Berlin, and therefore, as a free man, I take pride in the words *Ich bin ein Berliner* [I am a Berliner]."

President John F. Kennedy delivers his famous speech at the Berlin Wall on June 26, 1963.

Some 120,000 demonstrators march through the East German city of Leipzig on October 17, 1989, demanding greater freedom.

THE POLITICAL CONDITIONS THAT would eventually bring down the Berlin Wall began to develop in 1985, when Mikhail Gorbachev became leader of the Soviet Union. He wanted to introduce reform to the Soviet Union, while keeping it a communist state. Gorbachev introduced two striking new ideas: *glasnost*—freedom of information, free speech, and free elections, and *perestroika*—economic reform within communism. Significantly, he also began to withdraw Soviet control from the political systems of other Eastern Bloc countries. Gorbachev felt that they should experience reform without Soviet interference.

In June 1989, Gorbachev made his first visit to West Germany and was greeted by crowds of supporters. What newspapers across Europe were calling "Gorbymania" was an expression of hope that the Cold War might be coming to an end. When asked about the Berlin Wall, Gorbachev said: "The wall could disappear once the conditions that created the need for it disappeared." He was saying that the fall of the wall was dependent on the end of the Cold War.

Also in June, Poland elected a non-communist government. Nothing like this had happened before in an Eastern Bloc country under Soviet influence. Even more dramatic was Hungary's decision, on September 10, 1989, to allow East German refugees to cross the Hungarian border into Austria. Many East Germans had traveled to Hungary during the summer and waited at the border in the hope that this would happen. Now they drove across Austria and into West Germany. The Iron Curtain was being raised.

The East German government was facing a crisis. Protesters gathered in the city of Leipzig, calling for an end to laws that prevented them from traveling freely into the West. In the East German city of Dresden, young people took over the railroad station in an attempt to ride out of the country on a train.

In October 1989, Gorbachev visited East Berlin to help celebrate the 40th anniversary of the founding of East Germany. Also present was Erich Honecker, the hard-line communist leader of East Germany. Honecker was strongly opposed to Gorbachev's reforms. At a torchlight parade intended to celebrate East German power, marchers chanted, "Gorby, Gorby, save us!"

Honecker had lost control of the situation. Having also lost the support of Gorbachev, he was forced by the politburo to resign. They replaced him with Egon Krenz, another hard-line communist who was, however, prepared to make limited changes. By November, a million people were marching in the streets of East Berlin, demanding that the borders be opened. It was time for the wall to come down.

Mikhail Gorbachev (1931–)

Mikhail Gorbachev joined the Communist Party in 1952, and became local party leader in Stavropol in 1970. He was appointed agricultural secretary in 1978, and became a full member of the politburo two years later. In 1985, he became leader of the Soviet Union. Gorbachev hoped to revive the failing Soviet economy by changing some aspects of communism while maintaining its basic beliefs. He also abandoned the Soviet policy of intervening in any communist state that needed help to maintain communism. This was an essential step in the eventual fall of the Berlin Wall.

The parade to celebrate the 40th anniversary of East Germany on October 7, 1989, which was watched by Gorbachev and Honecker.

East Berliners climb up onto the Berlin Wall on the night of November 9–10, 1989.

O N THURSDAY, NOVEMBER 9, 1989, the press conference described at the beginning of this book took place. The vital detail that travelers would be required to obtain visas was lost in the excitement of the main news: East Germans would be allowed to cross the border. Journalists ran from the room, most to the nearest telephone. Within the hour, East German television was broadcasting the news that the barriers along the Berlin Wall were opening. The switchboards were jammed by East Berliners unable to believe what they were hearing. When West German television also started to broadcast the news, people stepped out into the frosty Berlin night to see if it was true. At the wall itself, no one had given the East German guards new orders. They stayed at their posts as the crowds gathered at the wall's crossing points.

9:00 P.M. A few people approached the guards at the crossing point on Invaliden Strasse. The guards told them they would have to obtain passports and visas before they could cross.

9:30 P.M. A middle-aged husband and wife went to the Bornholmer Strasse crossing and asked to be allowed through. The guard there had heard the news on his radio. He let them through, but made them promise to come back to East Berlin later on! The crowd of East Berliners that had gathered behind them recovered from their amazement and approached the guard. He waved them all through.

10:30 P.M. Programs on West German television were interrupted as news crews arrived at the crossing points. Word spread that

East Germans in Trabant cars line up to cross the Glienicker Bridge into West Berlin.

people were going through at Bornholmer Strasse. The guards at the other official crossing points, confused and without official orders, heaved up the barriers—some of them rusted into place from disuse—and allowed the crowds through. On the other side of the wall, they met West Berliners who had come to greet them, carrying whatever they could pick up as gifts: hot drinks, flowers, and champagne.

11:59 P.M. — By midnight, the border guards had received official orders to open the gates. There were lines of East German Trabant cars at each crossing point, filled with East Berliners. Some were still wearing their pajamas. A street party broke out in West Berlin. Just after midnight, a young man climbed up on his friend's shoulders and clambered onto the wall. Only hours before, he might have been shot. Now the top of the wall became a sea of dancing figures, spraying champagne over the crowds below. Someone brought out some fireworks, and gaudy rockets began soaring over the celebrations.

A Narrow Escape

" We didn't get any instructions from our superiors, none. Only, 'observe the situation.' We tried many times to speak to our superiors, but nobody got back to us. You have to bear in mind that our soldiers were fully armed on this day as always. And they had one order [shoot anyone who tries to cross]. "

Lothar Stein, a guard on duty that night, recalls how the celebrations might have turned to tragedy. Quoted in the CNN television documentary The Wall Comes Down.

On the night of November 9, 1989, a celebration began on top of the Berlin Wall.

THE PARTY LASTED ALL through the early hours of Friday November 10, with about 40,000 East Berliners crossing to the West. Stores had stayed open all night, and many East Berliners went window-shopping. When they were tired they simply went home or slept in the parks. The wall, 10 feet (3 m) wide in some places, was crowded with dancers. All along it, there was the sound of hammers and crowbars chipping away at the stone. The noise expressed years of anger that the wall should ever have existed.

3:30 A.M. The East Berlin newspaper *Berliner Zeitung* was handed around on the streets bearing the headline: "The wall is gone. Berlin is Berlin again!"

9:00 A.M. At Eberswalder Platz, East Berlin, bulldozers demolished a section of the wall to make a new crossing. People decorated the

gap with flowers, and West Berliners flocked to it to welcome the "Ossis," as they called the East Berliners. At one crossing-point, British soldiers in charge of the barrier erected trestle-tables on which they put tea-urns and plates of cookies. In West Berlin, children were given the day off school.

Since September 1, 1987, the West German government had been offering visitors from East Germany a "welcome to the West" gift of 100 Deutsche marks. In 1989, this was worth about $55. It was enough to buy a few luxuries: fruit, candy, or some perfume. Long lines of East Berliners now formed at banks and money-changers in West Berlin to collect their money.

In the evening, East and West German border guards worked together to hold back the crowds so that no one would be injured in the crush. Some of the guards swapped hats. As they carried small children to safety

West Berliners begin to tear down the wall that had divided their city.

The Century's Business

" *We walked everywhere, watching whole slabs of the wall crash down, seeing flurries of celebration, awkward reunions, people falling silent. Then dawn came up. We breakfasted groggily on brandy, coffee, and pastries outside a cafe, under a crystal blue sky…it soon became clear that a lot of the century's business, and a dreadful period in Germany's history, was being concluded.* "

Henry Porter, an English student at the time, remembers the night of November 10, 1989. Quoted in the Guardian, November 2, 1999.

they complained to their former enemies about the foolish behavior of the crowds. News had traveled across the world and people from all over Europe had joined the throngs at the wall, cheering every East German Trabant as it sputtered across the border.

In the first 24 hours after the border was opened, only about 1,200 "Ossis" registered for permanent residence in West Berlin. For most people the opening of the wall was a symbol of change in their own country, not a chance to escape from it. One woman recalled her experience of a few hours in the West: "Going to West Berlin was as good as going to Australia for me. It was just as far away. But now I've been there and back while my children were home in bed."

A West Berlin policeman (left) offers a helping hand as his former enemy, an East Berlin guard, steps through a break in the wall.

An East German guard reaches up to hand a flower to West Berliners sitting on top of the wall.

East German vehicles with water cannon protect the Brandenburg Gate as the wall is constructed in 1961.

Achtung!
Sie verlassen jetzt
West - Berlin

The Brandenburg Gate

The Brandenburg Gate was built in a three-year period, from 1788 to 1791, as a symbol of peace, after Prussia—a German state—had intervened in the Netherlands to prevent a revolutionary uprising. But from such beginnings, it became a symbol of German nationalism and military power. It was at the Brandenburg Gate that Adolf Hitler staged many of the Nazis' political rallies. The great arch, with its statue of a chariot drawn by four horses, was destroyed in World War II. It was rebuilt in 1958, and in 1989 was at the heart of the German demonstrations supporting reunification. Sad to say, 10 years later it became a meeting point for neo-Nazi demonstrations.

IN THE DAYS SURROUNDING the momentous opening of the Berlin Wall, one particular place attracted the attention of protesters. Demonstrators calling for the reunification of Germany gathered at the famous arched gateway called the Brandenburg Gate. Until the Berlin Wall was built, the gate had been part of a main road in Berlin and traffic passed through it every day. Then, in 1961, the wall was built in front of it, leaving it in East Berlin, and the gate was closed to both East and West Berliners.

On the night of Friday November 10, 1989, West German protesters climbed up onto the top of the Berlin Wall opposite the Brandenburg Gate. There was a "no-man's-land" on the eastern side of the wall, which had been created to make it impossible for escapees to even reach the wall without being shot. Now, East Germans crossed this no-man's-land and were pulled up onto the wall by the West German protesters.

The East German border guards had the strange experience during the day of stopping people from getting into East Berlin rather than out of it. As the crowds built up around the Brandenburg Gate, more troops were sent in to keep demonstrators in order. Some 300 armed East German troops formed a barrier in front of the gate while truckloads of reinforcements waited behind it.

From time to time, East German troops fired watercannon at people dancing on the wall. Some West Berliners climbed over the wall and dropped down into the no-man's-land in front of the Brandenburg Gate. Every so often the guards drove them away. At 3:00 A.M., protesters broke off a piece of the wall in front of the gate, and both West and East German troops hurried in to clear the area.

For weeks after the Berlin Wall opened, crowds gathered around the gate, with car headlights lighting it from both sides. They called for its opening, until finally it was announced that the gate would be officially reopened on December 22, 1989. The news was met with mixed feelings by Germany's neighbors. Both Great Britain and France saw the event as part of a resurgence of the kind of nationalism that had led to the rise of the Nazis in the 1930s. President François Mitterrand of France —a country invaded and conquered by Nazi Germany—refused to attend the ceremony.

East German guards stand at the Brandenburg Gate on November 10, 1989, as West Germans gather to celebrate the fall of the Berlin Wall.

On Saturday, November 11, a crane lifts out an entire section of the wall to make a new crossing-point.

ON THE AFTERNOON OF Saturday November 11, 1989, the West Berlin soccer team Hertha Berlin was playing. East Berliners, who for 28 years had only been able to watch their team play on television, were offered free tickets. As the crowds flooded into West Berlin, more breaches were made in the wall to accommodate them. At one place in the wall the crowd knocked over an entire 10-foot-high(3-m) section of concrete and physically carried it away.

Overnight, maps of the city had been printed to help the Ossis find their way around. The Kurfurstendamm,

West Berlin's main shopping area, was closed to traffic. Soup kitchens had been set up, and shops, bars, and restaurants handed out gifts to the visitors. Banks ran out of cash for the "welcome to the West" handouts, stores ran out of fresh fruit, and the price of bananas rose by 10 percent. One chain of supermarkets had trucks driven up to the crossing-points to give out bags of sugar.

In the evening, the Berlin Philharmonic Orchestra performed a free concert in West Berlin, playing the music of the great German composer Ludwig van Beethoven. Outside of the city the borders between

Over the following months the wall was completely demolished by Prem and other contractors, and the pieces were carted away for road-building projects. In the 21st century, only one tiny section of the wall has been preserved as a reminder of its history.

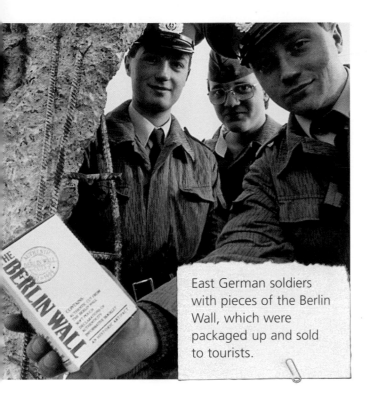

East German soldiers with pieces of the Berlin Wall, which were packaged up and sold to tourists.

A Moment in Time

Potsdammer Platz—once a bustling square at the centre of Berlin—has stood silent and empty for 28 years, lit only by the beams of searchlights. At 8:30 A.M., November 12, 1989, an entire section of the wall here is lifted out by crane. On either side of the gap stands a man. Walter Momper, the mayor of West Berlin, and Erhart Krack, the mayor of East Berlin, are waiting to formally greet each other. As the area is cleared, the two men step forward and meet in the square. They shake hands. Walter Momper announces that Potsdammer Platz will regain its former identity as a square at the heart of the reunified city. A roar goes up from the crowds.

East and West Germany had opened in places, and lines of cars waiting to cross stretched for more than 35 miles (60 km). All over Germany, beyond the joyful and exuberant partying at the wall, families met relatives they had not seen for 28 years. Many had not expected to see each other ever again. By midnight, two million people had crossed into West Berlin. Most of them simply returned home to their families and jobs the next morning.

On Sunday November 12, the West German government got over its own shock at what had happened and began making plans. It announced that East Germans could travel free on public transportation and could gain free entry to all public entertainment.

In the following week, bits of the wall were being hawked as souvenirs, and builders made a profitable trade out of demolishing further sections to allow more freedom of access. One West German demolition contractor, named Winifried Prem, said he had always dreamed of "how my crushing machine could crumple and pulverize the wall." Now he realized his dream.

Mayors Walter Momper and Erhart Krack shake hands in Potsdammer Platz, on November 12.

West German chancellor Helmut Kohl lends his support to the East German elections in March 1990.

Free Elections

In March 1990, free elections were held in East Germany for the first time, to elect a national assembly and government. The party that won was supported by Chancellor Kohl's party in West Germany. An East German expressed his voting intention: "Kohl's is the party of money, so I'm voting for it."

THE BERLIN WALL HAD symbolized the divisions of the Cold War, which had seen the German people split into two separate nations and kept apart by force. The tearing down of the wall represented the end of this Cold War conflict, but it also raised a vital question. What would happen now to the two Germanys?

Even before the end of November 1989, the chancellor of West Germany, Helmut Kohl, announced his government's wish to reunite the two Germanys. New elections were due in West Germany in December

1990, and Kohl wanted to win these elections by leading the way in the reunification of Germany. The United States supported the idea, with the condition that a united Germany must become part of the Western system of democracy.

The possibility that the two parts of Germany would once again form a united country alarmed some people. For many East Germans, who had taken part in the demonstrations in Leipzig and East Berlin before the wall fell, reunification was an unexpected result. Like Gorbachev, many of the demonstrators were committed communists. They just saw no reason why communists should not have free elections and freedom of speech, as well as the things they were used to having, such as subsidized housing, free healthcare, and full employment. On their visits to the West, East Berliners saw fresh fruit, electronic goods, designer labels and perfumed soap. But they also saw things that were not so attractive, such as the enormous gap between the wealthy and the poor.

West Germans, especially West Berliners, also saw problems ahead. Their streets were filled with noisy, polluting East German Trabants or "Trabbie" cars.

Their stores were crowded. Levels of petty crime had soared, and there was a shortage of housing and food. East Germany had a number of serious economic and environmental problems. Its industries were so old-fashioned that some machinery was bought up immediately by museums. Industry had also not had strict laws for waste disposal. Any West German business that chose to form links with an East German company faced huge expenses in cleaning up the environmental pollution.

Kohl foresaw many of these problems. Very quickly after the wall fell, he also proposed a common currency, assuring the people of both halves of Germany that there would be no loss to either side. A special rate would be set between the two currencies so that East Germans, whose currency was so much weaker, would not have their savings wiped out by a poor exchange rate.

East Berliners protest against reunification.

In July 1990, Mikhail Gorbachev and Helmut Kohl signed agreements allowing the united Germany to become a free and independent state.

B Y THE TIME OF East Germany's free elections in March 1990, it had become generally accepted that Germany would be reunified. It had also become obvious that West Germany, with its economic power, would be in charge of events. East Germany would be a willing but less powerful participant.

The meetings that led to the reunification of Germany took place between May and September, 1990. The two Germanys negotiated their future with the four powers that had agreed to the partition of Germany and Berlin after World War II: the United States, the Soviet Union, Great Britain, and France. According to treaties signed after the war, these four powers still had certain rights over Germany. From the negotiations emerged the "Two-Plus-Four" Treaty. The West German foreign minister Hans Dietrich Genscher, who came up with the term, explained: "We had to avoid giving the impression that the Four were

negotiating about Germany. This is how the word order in the title of the conference came about: Two plus Four, not Four plus Two."

The Soviet Union played a crucial role in deciding on the nature of a new, united Germany. In July 1990, at the same time as the German currency union was taking place, Gorbachev and Kohl held talks. As a result, Gorbachev agreed that a united Germany should be a free and independent state. This meant the country would have the right to join NATO (North Atlantic Treaty Organization)—the military alliance, led by the United States, that had opposed the Soviet Union during the Cold War.

Kohl announced, at a press conference on July 16, 1990, that a reunified Germany would be part of NATO. This caused almost as much astonishment as the press statement made seven months earlier, when

Schabowski had announced that East Berliners could cross the Berlin Wall. Not only was the Cold War over, but it felt to some as if the United States had won. On October 3, 1990, a new Germany came into existence, in which East and West Germany, and East and West Berlin, were combined.

Not everyone welcomed the prospect of a unified Germany. France's President François Mitterrand and the British prime minister Margaret Thatcher had opposed the idea. They shared a fear among Germany's wartime enemies that a powerful German state might once again dominate Europe.

For Germans themselves, there were immediate problems. Those from the east had no experience of competing for work. They also had none of the technical skills needed to compete for jobs.

Immigrants from all over Eastern Europe were also seeking a better life in Germany. This led to the growth of pro-Nazi groups, who wished to keep their new country for themselves.

A Changing Berlin

" For me and other members of my generation it was comfortable not to have…Germany any more. So I could say I had nothing to do with the Germany of the concentration camps and the Holocaust. The Federal Republic I grew up in was not Germany, only West Germany… over all those years I had built up an… anti-German identity. And then these refugees arrived calling out 'Deutschland' from the train windows. "

Sociologist Wolf Wagner on how reunification forced the postwar generation to face up to their country's past. Quoted in Unchained Eagle: Germany After the Wall *by Tom Henegan (Reuters, 2000).*

Another moment of history at the Brandenburg Gate: a fireworks display to celebrate German reunification on October 3, 1990.

Stasi secret police struggle with a demonstrator protesting at the celebrations of East Germany's 40th anniversary on October 7, 1989.

IN THE MONTHS FOLLOWING the fall of the wall, there were many revelations about how East Germany had been run. Evidence emerged of corruption among the politicians who had once controlled the state, and of the brutal behavior of East Germany's secret police, the Stasi.

In former East Berlin, people attacked the Stasi offices, and took away any secret files that had not been hidden or destroyed. These files revealed that there had been 85,000 full-time employees of the Stasi, and over half a million paid informants. These informants had spied on their neighbors and fellow workers, and reported any suspicious behavior to the Stasi. The Stasi had kept files on the activities of a third of all East German citizens.

All Germans were now permitted to see their own files. Some had the unpleasant shock of finding out that close family members had been spying on them. Where it was possible, Stasi informants and employees were now fired from their jobs. But informing had been carried out on such a huge scale that most informants escaped punishment. Ex-members of the Stasi also found it easy to accuse their enemies of having once worked for them. Justice was hard to achieve, and a great deal of bitterness was aroused.

Other revelations showed up the double standards of the former East German leaders. Although they claimed to despise Western luxuries, many had enjoyed goods unavailable to the public. Erich Honecker, East Germany's leader from 1973 to 1989,

An employee at Stasi headquarters in Berlin looks through the files that have been opened to public inspection.

Learning the Truth

" I was brought up and educated by that regime. I never knew anything else. I truly believed it was right. I trusted my party and my government and I genuinely thought the Stasi were doing a good job to protect society —until two or three years ago when the stories of their brutalities began to leak out, but at first I just didn't believe them.... Now I feel bereft. But I still believe in the socialist ideal. "

An East German journalist describes how the revelations affected him. Quoted in Germany and the Germans *by John Ardagh.*

had owned a hunting lodge with a staff of 22 people, as well as an island retreat in the Baltic Sea. He and his wife had even made secret trips to Paris to go shopping. Such luxuries were normal for political leaders in the West, but Honecker was a communist leader who claimed to believe in equality. Senior politicians in Honecker's government were also accused of selling arms to foreign countries in order to fund their private bank accounts.

Officials had been responsible for ordering the killing of people who tried to escape across the Berlin Wall. But they could not easily be prosecuted, since they had acted under East German law. As the 1990s progressed, some former ministers and members of the Stasi were brought to trial, but little was proved. Honecker, now an elderly man, was arrested and charged with corruption and manslaughter. However, he was allowed later to leave Germany when he became ill. He went first to Russia, and then to Chile, where he died in 1994.

Erich Honecker is extradited from Moscow to Germany to stand trial for his part in the deaths at the Berlin Wall.

IN THE FIRST YEARS after the wall fell, there were many problems in Germany. Berlin in particular needed massive redevelopment. Large areas of housing in East Berlin were in poor condition. The old center of the city, where the wall had been, had become a no-man's-land. The city's leaders also had a unique problem: they had to coordinate two healthcare systems, two education systems, two public transportation systems, and so on.

In 1961 East Berlin's subway, known as the U-bahn, had been cut off from the West for fear that East Berliners might escape through the tunnels. In 1989, fifteen stations were reopened, along with roads and bridges. But telephone lines were very limited and those in East Berlin were outdated. In the months following reunification, little could be done to modernize them.

In the arts there were more than two of everything. The governments of East and West Berlin had poured money into the arts to show off their city. There were three opera houses, ten orchestras, twenty-seven theaters and three world-class museum complexes. These had to be sorted out, into what was and was not essential. This generally meant that jobs had to be cut in the overstaffed theaters of East Berlin.

Wildlife along the Wall

For 28 years, a strip of land 300 feet (90 m) wide and 27 miles (43 km) long had been left undisturbed in the heart of Berlin—where the wall had stood. Much of this land ran along railroad lines and through parks. When the land-mines, the barbed wire, and the wall itself had been cleared away, biologists discovered that the area contained unexpected flora and fauna. There were 1,432 species of plants and animals along the strip, five times more than the average for other cities. Kingfishers were well established there, as were plants that usually grow in warmer climates. It is thought that seeds and insects were accidentally brought in along the railroad lines and grew in the undisturbed environment. Sad to say, most of this environment has now disappeared in the huge rebuilding projects of the city center.

Inside the Theater Unter den Linden, one of East Berlin's many theaters.

This new dome was built on top of the Reichstag in 1996, after it became Germany's new legislative building,

The main debate to concern the German government was whether Berlin should now become the country's capital again. The city still had the grand old buildings of prewar Germany. These included the Reichstag, or parliament building; St. Nicholas Church, built in 1200; many beautiful museum buildings; and the Brandenburg Gate. Berlin also had a huge area of free land where the wall had stood, which would make a perfect site for grand new public buildings. However, Berlin also brought with it memories of the Nazi era, and of the kind of nationalism that had once threatened to destroy the whole of Europe.

The other option was the city of Bonn. It had been the capital of West Germany, and Germany's allies in NATO were familiar with the city as a place where they discussed trade, European integration, and other peacetime events. However, Bonn was located in the west of the unified country. It would make East Germans feel even more unimportant.

In 1991 it was finally decided to make Berlin the capital. The decision was made even though it meant moving all the government offices and the parliament building from one side of the country to the other.

Past and present in Berlin: A replica of the world's first traffic signals of 1924, outside the Red Box, a building in which plans for the city's future are put on display for the public.

Mikhail Gorbachev was declared *Time* magazine's "Man of the Decade" for the 1980s.

WHILE GERMAN REUNIFICATION gathered pace, the rest of the world watched open-mouthed as changes it had never thought possible took place in Europe. The fall of the Berlin Wall had signaled the end of the Cold War, and the consequences of this momentous event reached far beyond the borders of Germany.

In Eastern Europe, communist governments quickly gave way to democracies. Czechoslovakia, Poland, and Hungary made the transition to democratic government with little violence. But in Romania it was a very different story. The communist leaders of Romania refused to give up their power without a struggle. There was a coup, and the communist dictator Nicolae Ceausescu and his wife were executed by firing squad.

The peaceful end of the Cold War was Mikhail Gorbachev's greatest achievement, but he and his country were to pay a very high price for this extraordinary event. The most unexpected consequence was the collapse of the Soviet Union itself. Non-Russian states within the Soviet Union, such as Lithuania and Latvia, began calling for their independence. A Russian leader, Boris Yeltsin, supported them and challenged Gorbachev's position as leader of the Soviet Union. On Christmas Day 1991, Gorbachev accepted that the Soviet Union had come to an end, and resigned as its leader. Yeltsin then became head of the new state of Russia.

Events such as the fall of the Berlin Wall seemed to many to represent not just the end of the Cold War but the victory of the United States in that conflict.

Some Russians, without wishing to resurrect the Cold War, felt a sense of humiliation and defeat at the loss of their country's superpower status. Others, like Yeltsin, wanted Russia to embrace capitalism in ways that Gorbachev had never intended. As the new millennium began, Russia was striving to cope with the frantic pace of its economic reforms, and to find a new role for itself in the world.

Many people believed that the end of the Cold War would create a period of peace in Europe. This did not happen. The former Yugoslavia, in particular, has suffered many crises. Yugoslavia had been created as a country at the end of World War I, and it held together states including Bosnia, Croatia, and Serbia. In 1991, as the Soviet Union broke up, these states began to demand their own independence. Within months, a war had broken out among different ethnic groups— a war marked by terrible atrocities.

Celebrate or Forget?

The Germany that emerged after the fall of the Berlin Wall faced new problems and challenges. So did the new independent states that emerged after the end of the Cold War. This German joke, from 1999, reflects the mixed emotions felt in Germany and Europe:

Customer: "Waiter, what wine do you recommend for the tenth anniversary of German unity?"
Waiter: "That depends..."
Customer: "On what?"
Waiter: "Well, do you want to celebrate or forget?"

Quoted in Along the Wall and Watchtowers *by Oliver August.*

Refugees in 1999 flee from fighting in Serbia, in the former Yugoslavia. The end of the Soviet Union brought war and misery to the region.

Soviet tanks end the Prague Spring of 1968. If the Berlin Wall had not fallen, would Soviet tanks have crushed the protests in East Germany in the same way?

WHAT IF, ON NOVEMBER 10, 1989, the East German or Soviet governments had acted to prevent the fall of the Berlin Wall? How might history have been different?

In East Germany before the wall came down, there had been demonstrations by thousands of people demanding freedom to travel and free elections. Erich Honecker had ordered security police to open fire on protesters in Leipzig in October 1989, but local leaders had disobeyed him. If they had not, there could have been terrible bloodshed. A similar situation had ended in violence in communist China a few months earlier. In June 1989, large crowds of demonstrators had gathered in Tiananmen Square, in the Chinese capital of Beijing, and called on the communist government to relax its authoritarian rule.

The Chinese authorities ordered troops to open fire, killing hundreds of people.

Had the wall not come down, more and more East Germans would have fled to the West. The East German economy, already failing, might have collapsed as factories and offices emptied of workers. In such a situation, the East German government might have tried to prevent the mass emigrations by using military force at the Berlin Wall. The East Germans might then have called on Soviet forces for support. This had happened in Czechoslovakia during the Prague Spring of 1968, when reforms had been ended by the arrival of Soviet tanks. But by 1989, the attitude of the Soviet Union toward the communist countries of the Eastern Bloc had softened.

The Berlin Wall might also have fallen in a less dramatic way, with the two halves of Germany agreeing to remain apart but on friendly terms. West Germany experienced an economic slump as it took on the East German economy. This might have been prevented if Germany had remained divided. East Germany might eventually have joined the European Union on its own, as Poland and other East European countries were preparing to do at the beginning of the new millennium. Some people feel that Germany is now too much of a force. They think it would have been better to have two smaller countries in the center of Europe—an independent West Germany and an independent East Germany.

It is also quite possible to argue that the opening of the wall was just one small, if dramatic, consequence of the broader reforms taking place across Eastern Europe. If the wall had not fallen in the way it did, the broader changes might well have happened anyway—and eventually the wall might simply have ceased to function as a barrier dividing Berlin.

Unforgotten

" Unforgotten are
Those murdered on the border
Chiselled in stone
Their names live on
Imprinted on the memory
The image lives on. "

Part of a poem written by an East German border guard, mourning the East German guards killed by those seeking to escape. It could equally apply to the many escapees who were shot while trying to escape.

Quoted in Along the Wall and Watchtowers *by Oliver August.*

Chinese tanks confront a demonstrator in Tiananmen Square, Beijing, in June 1989. Erich Honecker had called unsuccessfully for a similar show of force to keep the Berlin Wall intact.

Ten years after the fall of the Berlin Wall, (left to right) German chancellor Helmut Kohl, Soviet premier Mikhail Gorbachev, and American president George Bush sign a piece of the wall.

MORE THAN A DECADE after the events of November 9, 1989, it is possible to look back on the fall of the Berlin Wall and put it in perspective. As a symbol of the end of the Cold War, the fall of the wall was a key moment in the history of Europe. With Europe no longer divided into East and West, expansion of both the European Union and NATO was able to gather pace.

Some people still have concerns about the influence of a reunited Germany within the European Union. They are afraid that Germany is now too powerful a member. For others, though, the opposite is true. They look to a united Europe as the best way of ensuring peace. In the past, disputes were settled on battlefields with rival armies and deadly weapons; or by building a wall and guarding it with soldiers under orders to shoot anyone trying to get across. Within a united Europe, with a common set of laws, there may be a greater chance that governments will be able to settle conflicts peacefully.

In Germany itself, the legacy of the opening of the wall has been a mixed one. The initial problems have grown fewer, but the former East Germany continues to be far poorer than the western half of the country. Since 1989 some old destructive ideas have also reemerged, especially in the east. On a number of occasions neo-Nazi groups have launched racist attacks against immigrant workers. This has raised fears of a return to the nationalism in Germany that brought Adolf Hitler to power.

Finally, with the end of the Cold War the balance of power in the world has changed. The fall of the Berlin Wall may be seen not just as the end of a divided Germany. It also represents the end of a world held in an uneasy truce between the nuclear threats of two superpowers, the United States and the Soviet Union. This balance of power was a perilous one, but it also prevented either superpower from dominating world events.

German police search a neo-Nazi demonstrator during a march in Berlin on March 12, 2000.

With the reunification of Germany and the collapse of the Soviet Union, Europe is no longer divided into two hostile groups. Perhaps the final legacy of the fall of the Berlin Wall is the possibility that Europe could become independent of any superpower. In this case, it may be possible for a more peaceful Europe to develop.

Looking Back

"The wall is open...are you kidding? Are you kidding? Everyone knew it was true, but you couldn't quite believe it. We thought we would wake up in the morning and nobody is in the country."

Wolfreida Schmidt, an actor in the Volksbuhne, or People's Theater, remembers the day she heard the news that the Berlin Wall had fallen.

The start of the new millennium is celebrated at the Brandenburg Gate.

Glossary

airlift The transportation of supplies by air, especially in an emergency.

alliance A group of nations that have agreed to help each other, particularly in war.

Allies The group of nations that fought against Nazi Germany in World War II.

authoritarian Ruling by force, rather than electing representatives.

blockade The surrounding and cutting off of a place, to prevent goods or people from entering or leaving.

buffer state A country that acts as a barrier between two other countries to stop them from going to war.

capitalism An economic and political system in which industry is owned and managed by individuals, whose chief motive is making profit.

Cold War The confrontation that set the Soviet Union and its allies in Eastern Europe against the United States and its allies in Western Europe. The Cold War lasted from 1945 until 1989.

communism An economic and political system in which there is no private ownership of property and in which the economy is owned by and managed by the state—whose aim is to provide for its citizens rather than make a profit.

concentration camps Camps for holding political prisoners, especially those run by Nazi Germany.

coup The overthrow of a government.

currency union The merger of two or more currencies.

democracy Government by all the people, through their fairly elected representatives.

dictator A powerful individual who rules a country by force.

Eastern Bloc The communist countries of Eastern Europe that were under the control of the Soviet Union.

economic system The way in which wealth is produced and distributed in a country.

emigrate To leave one country to settle in another.

European Union An organization of European nations that cooperate in the areas of politics, economics, law enforcement, immigration, and military security.

exchange rate The comparative values of currencies from different nations.

immigrants People who come to live permanently in a new country after having left their home country.

informants People who pass on information, often in secret and to the police.

Iron Curtain An expression used to describe the border that separated the communist countries of Eastern Europe and the democratic, capitalist countries of Western Europe.

liberal Supporting democratic reform and greater personal freedom.

military service Compulsory or voluntary service in the armed forces.

money-changers People who change money from one currency into another.

national assembly A group of elected representatives who decide on a country's laws.

nationalism Taking pride in one's nationality and country and supporting one's own national culture and interests, often at the expense of other countries.

NATO (North Atlantic Treaty Organization) A military alliance between the United States and its allies, set up in 1949.

Nazis The political party that brought Adolf Hitler to power in Germany.

neo-Nazi Reviving the attitudes of the Nazis, such as nationalism and racism.

no-man's-land A piece of disputed land between two opposing armies, or the waste area on either side of a military barrier such as the Berlin Wall.

"Ossis" The West Germans' nickname for East Germans (from the German *ost*, meaning east).

partition Dividing up of a country into regions with separate governments.

politburo In communist countries, the central committee of politicians that made the decisions about how to run the country.

Prussia A central European state with Berlin as its capital, which existed before the unification of Germany in 1871.

rat race An expression meaning the struggle for power in everyday life.

redevelopment The building of new houses, and creation of new industry, in an area where these have decayed.

reform Developments and improvements, especially those that change and improve political systems.

reunification Reuniting the parts of a once-divided country.

socialist Having the political belief that communities, rather than individuals, should own the means to produce, distribute, and exchange goods.

Soviet Union Also called the USSR (Union of Soviet Socialist Republics), the Soviet Union was officially created in 1922, and was the world's first communist country.

subsidized Supported by money from the government.

superpower An extremely powerful country, especially the United States and the Soviet Union during the Cold War.

trade union An organization of workers that exists to protect their rights.

visa A document or pass allowing somebody to enter a foreign country.

Further Information

Reading

Degens, T. *Freya on the Wall*. New York: Harcourt Inc., 1997.

Grant, R. G. *New Perspectives: The Berlin Wall*. New York: Raintree Steck-Vaughn Publishers, 1998.

Kelly, Nigel. *The Fall of the Berlin Wall: The Cold War Ends (Point of Impact)*. Chicago, IL: Heinemann Library, 2001.

Lutzeier, Elizabeth. *The Wall*. New York: Holiday House Inc., 1992.

Films

Fall of the Berlin Wall directed by Peter Claus Schmidt (1990).

Roger Waters: The Wall, Live in Berlin directed by Roger Waters and Ken O'Neil (1989).

Time Line

May 7, 1945 Nazi Germany surrenders to the Allies. Soviets troops occupy Berlin.

July 3, 1945 Berlin is divided into four sectors – Soviet, American, French, and British.

June 30, 1946 The border between East and West Berlin is guarded.

June 1948–May 1949 The Soviet blockade of Berlin and the Berlin airlift.

April 4, 1949 The North Atlantic Treaty Organization (NATO) is formed.

May 24, 1949 The Federal Republic of Germany (West Germany) is founded.

October 7, 1949 The German Democratic Republic (East Germany) is founded.

May 26, 1952 The border between East and West Germany is closed.

June 1953 Troops put down an uprising in East Berlin.

November 1956 A revolution in Hungary is put down by Soviet troops.

December 11, 1957 Leaving East Germany without permission becomes a crime punishable by three years in prison.

August 13, 1961 The Berlin Wall is built.

August 17, 1962 Peter Fechter becomes the first person to be killed while trying to cross the Berlin Wall.

June 26, 1963 President John F. Kennedy makes a famous speech in West Berlin.

August 1968 Czechoslovakia's revolution, known as the "Prague Spring," is put down by Soviet tanks.

August 31, 1980 Solidarity, a trade union in Poland, is officially recognized.

March 11, 1985 Mikhail Gorbachev becomes leader of the Soviet Union.

September 10, 1989 East Germans cross the Hungarian border into Austria.

September 12, 1989 A freely elected government takes power in Poland.

October 7, 1989 Gorbachev attends the celebration of the 40th anniversary of East Germany.

October 18, 1989 Erich Honecker is forced to resign as leader of East Germany.

November 9, 1989 The crossing-points in the Berlin Wall are opened.

December 25, 1989 A coup in Romania ends the dictatorship of Nicolae Ceausescu.

July 1, 1990 Currency union between East and West Germany.

October 3, 1990 The reunification of Germany.

December 25, 1991 The Soviet Union is disbanded. Gorbachev resigns.

A memorial to Ottfried Reck, who died trying to cross the Berlin Wall in 1962.

Index

Numbers in **bold** refer
to illustrations and photographs.

GET TOOLED UP WITH THE STONE AGE SENTINEL

IT'S A MAMMOTH READ!

Cavemates!

Ed Zog here with four million years' worth of history, all crammed into a rock-melting 32 pages!

This here is the STONE AGE SENTINEL, and it's translated from the original Caveman for your comfort and convenience.

HOT

So what have we got? First of all we've got 18 pages of the hottest news this side of an erupting volcano. We start with

the first hominids to walk on two legs rather than four. (What's a hominid? You are, bone brain, and so are any of your ape-man predecessors!)

SWEAT

Read on and find out why bigger brains are best, why sweating is no bad thing, and why fire is the greatest thing since sliced mammoth.

Officially the Stone Age lasts from around 2,000,000 to 2,000 BC. But as we cover much more – from 4,000,000 to 2,000 BC – you're getting more years for your money than any other comparable newspaper!!!

WHAT'S THE CATCH?

And that's not all.

Want to know how to catch a mate Stone Age style?

Curious about what's cooking in the Stone Age stockpot?

Itching to find out what gets them grooving on the Stone Age dance floor?

Read our features between pages 20 and 32!

And remember, if it ain't stone, it ain't worth a bone!!!

Your pal

ed zog

Ed Zog, Editor,
Stone Age Sentinel

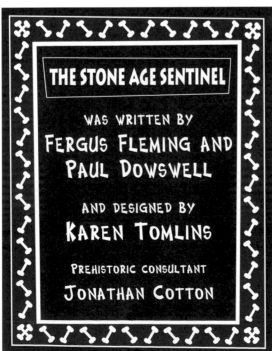

THE STONE AGE SENTINEL

WAS WRITTEN BY
FERGUS FLEMING AND PAUL DOWSWELL

AND DESIGNED BY
KAREN TOMLINS

PREHISTORIC CONSULTANT
JONATHAN COTTON

ARE YOU A MAN
OR A MOUSE?

Want to know where you come from? Look at the *Sentinel*'s easy-to-follow family tree and you'll see in a second how you fit into the evolutionary scheme of things...

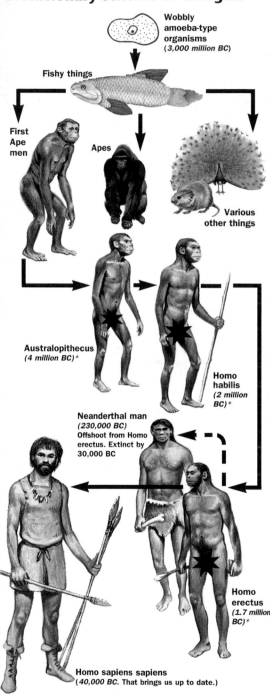

Wobbly amoeba-type organisms
(*3,000 million BC*)

Fishy things

First Ape men

Apes

Various other things

Australopithecus
(*4 million BC*)*

Homo habilis
(*2 million BC*)*

Neanderthal man
(*230,000 BC*)
Offshoot from Homo erectus. Extinct by 30,000 BC

Homo erectus
(*1.7 million BC*)*

Homo sapiens sapiens
(*40,000 BC*. That brings us up to date.)

So there you have it. From blob of jelly to modern man in a mere 3,000 million years. So whether you're an Australopithecus or a Homo erectus (or even a mouse), just remember, the *Sentinel* is FIRST WITH THE NEWS!!

TWO LEGS BETTER
THAN FOUR

Ape-man in "walking" sensation

4,000,000 BC

Is it a shoe or is it a glove? The age-old debate is over, according to evolutionary whiz-kids *Australopithecus*. From now on, say these ape-men, we don't have to go around on all fours. Instead we can walk upright.

FURROW

The brow-furrowing breakthrough came when this bunch of hominids realized the advantages of standing on two feet.

"It makes us nimbler and faster," said a two-legged spokesman. "It also makes us more versatile – we can carry things and run at the same time, for example. But above all, it gives us a very satisfying impression of height. When you walk on two feet you can peer over bushes, gaze manfully into the distance and grab things from high branches. None of this was possible on all fours."

THICK

"Naturally, we will retain some of our earlier characteristics – thick brows, massive jaws, long, strong arms, a tendency to stoop, and awkward table manners – but these will iron themselves out with the passage of time."

Standing a full 1.4m (4¹⁄₂ft) high, and weighing in at 27kg (60lb), *Australopithecus* (or "New Ape-Man") is more than able to cope with the demands of his environment.

Some *Australopithecus*es show off their two-legged skills. "They'll be dancing *Swan Lake* next," sneer rival species.

REELING

Apes who still walk on all four limbs are seriously worried for their future. "It's left us reeling!" said a representative of all-fours pressure group 'Can't Stand, Won't Stand.' "There we were, minding our own business, when these lanky streaks came darting past on two legs. It spoiled our day.

"We've tried copying them, but we just can't get the hang of it. They say it's like riding a bicycle: once you've learned, you never forget. What nonsense! And what's a bicycle anyway? Take it from me: two legs are downright unnatural!"

Our Getting-Around Correspondent, Larry Plunck says: "Walking is just the tip of the iceberg. Very soon we'll be able to amble, stroll, tiptoe, skip, march and dance the gavotte. The possibilities are endless."

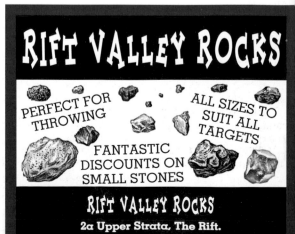
*The Sentinel is a respectable family newspaper and does not approve of nudity in any era.

ROCK ON!
IT'S THE STONE AGE!

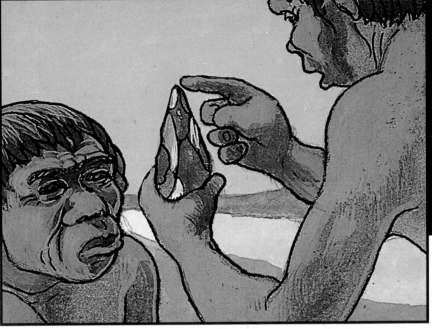

Homo habilis **invents the ancestor of the variable-speed power drill.**

THUMBS-UP TOOL TRICK GIVES HUMANS A HELPING HAND

2,000,000 BC

Watch out! There's a new idea about! That's the buzz around the African grassland as *Homo habilis*, the first recognizable human, saunters forth with his amazing new invention – the tool!

"Ever since we realized we didn't have to walk on our hands, we've been wondering what to do with our 'front feet'," a *Homo habilis* told us. "At last we've found the answer. After much experimentation we discovered that the twiddly parts at the end – now known as fingers – are not only great for picking berries and noses, but can also be used to make tools!

Tools? We asked top handyman Reggie Lugg to explain.

"Well, you see, a tool is something that does something better than hands – like scissors, dental floss and variable-speed drills with hammer-action for solid walls. Of course, we haven't invented these things yet, but we've made a respectable start by chipping stones to give them a sharp edge. On their own, sharp stones make very good knives. But tie a piece of wood onto them and you've got an axe, or even a spear!"

HACKING

Habilis means "skilled", and there's no doubt that *Homo habilis* is living up to his name. He's chipping and hacking like there's no tomorrow. In fact, he looks set to take over the whole world!

Ape-man *Australopithecus* is resigned to extinction. But they've got a few points to raise before they go.

"These new hominids may be clever, but they're a messy bunch," said one ape-person. "They leave their little shards of sharpened stone lying all over the place. What if our kids cut themselves on one of these things? We've still got another 800,000 years to go before we die out, so we think they ought to be more considerate. I'll bet people will still be picking up their mess millions of years from now."

Pleased to meat you!

Hunter-gatherers Come Out Top As Meat Mania Sweeps Globe

2,000,000 BC

It's Pick 'n' Mix time for us hominids as we face up to a brand new menu. Until now, we've had to content ourselves with picking berries, roots and the odd vegetable. Thanks to *Homo habilis*, however, a new item has been added to the menu – meat!

RUM

"Blearggh! Can't stand the stuff! Give me a nice rummage in the shrubs," said top *Australopithecus* ape-man and vegetarian, Ronnie Lurch.

But veggies like Lurch are up against stiff competition. Almost every kind of animal, from a gazelle to a quagga*, can find green stuff and eat it quicker than ape-men can. The only way to survive is to eat meat as well as veg.

GO FORTH

"It's all very well saying to go forth and gather," said leading *Homo habilis* Cornelius Gogg. "But in today's competitive environment you need to hunt too. That's why we're carving a niche for ourselves as hunter-gatherers."

The new breed of hunter-gatherers have set themselves a strict agenda. They've got a month in each area to strip all available vegetation, kill whatever they can, and then move on

This stuff is packed full of protein and is very tasty! It's more difficult to catch than a plant, but experts say it's definitely worth the extra effort.

to new ground.

Ape-men have responded with a detailed manifesto called 'Veg Is Best'. But their pledge that 'Brussel Sprouts Taste Nice' has been greeted with widespread derision.

*Modern-day hunter-gatherers please note: a quagga is a washed-out zebra which disappeared around AD 1900, so don't bother looking for it now.

3

THINK BIG

Here we go, here we go! A bunch of burly hom-inids flex those all important brain muscles.

SIZE MATTERS, SAY BRAIN GURUS

2,000,000 BC

A brain may not appear as immediately useful as a good set of teeth," head expert Professor Elmer Yarg said yesterday, "but it's indispensable if you want to get ahead in life. And research has shown that the bigger it is, the better you'll do."

LACK

Prof. Yarg and his colleagues claim that big brains make up for our lack of fangs, talons, tusks, claws, poison glands and other frightening things.

"If you have a big brain you can outwit creatures with smaller brains," said Prof. Yarg. "It's that simple. And as humans have got the biggest brains in the world we can outwit anything.

"Physically, we're weak and vulnerable. But we've got it up top and that's what counts. I wouldn't be surprised if we became the leading creatures on the planet."

AHEM

Opponents have slammed the big-brain theory on the grounds that human female's birth canals are not big enough to deliver children with big brains.

Prof. Yarg has the answer. "It's very straight-forward. What happens is that we're born with small brains and then they increase in size as we grow older. Other species do this, but they don't do it as well as we do. A human baby's brain is 25% of what it will be in adulthood. A chimpanzee, by comparison, is born with 65% of its total brain power."

(Adult human brains are almost twice as big as chimpanzees and by the 20th century AD they'll be three times as big. Wow!)

"Granted, there are some drawbacks. While the baby's brain is growing, it's completely dependent on its parents. A baboon can look after itself after 12 months whereas it takes a good six years for human kids to get the hang of things. So that means an awful lot more time and effort for the parents."

BRAIN OR BRAWN?

Decide for yourself which is best with our handy check list!

MAN	TIGER

Small	Big and hairy
Weedy little fingers	Fangs-and-all
Thinks	Roars
Sharpens Arrows	Sharpens Claws
Gets Friends	Gets Irritable
Makes Ambush	Makes Terrifying Faces
Home Before Dinner	Is dinner

HERE AT THE SENTINEL WE SAY THERE'S NO CONTEST!!! IT LOOKS LIKE THE BRAIN IS THE DEADLIEST WEAPON OF ALL.

PERSPIRATION? NO SWEAT!

MAN CHILLS OUT

2,000,000 BC

Do your smelly armpits embarrass you? Well don't you worry. According to the latest evidence, sweating buckets is a major bonus.

Dr. Oscar Snig explains all:

"Living as we do in Africa, it is vital to be able to keep cool. The basic way of doing this for most species is to lie in the shade, put out your tongue and pant. But this makes you look silly and is only effective in short bursts. If you do it on the run, you get dizzy and fall over – not to mention finding your mouth full of flies. That's why all the big predators tend not to do much round about midday."

LYING IN THE SUN

'Humans can't afford to lie around, especially at midday when the pickings'll be good, since the other carnivores are out of the way. So we've come up with two classy ways of keeping cool AND being able to hunt at the same time. First of all, we've lost most of our body hair. And secondly, we've learned how to sweat.

"Sweating is an incredibly efficient form of temperature control. The moment you get too hot, your body oozes water which cools you by evaporation. This means you can chase those pesky gazelles without having to stop every few minutes for a pant."

EXCESS

However, Snig warns, excess perspiration can be dangerous. Humans can only tolerate water loss amounting to 10% of their total body weight. Overly-enthusiastic sweaters run a risk of becoming dehydrated.

"It's very important to replace lost fluid. Some animals can store water very effectively – a camel, for example, can take aboard about 20 buckets of water in 10 minutes. Humans can only store a hundredth of that in the same time. Therefore I'd advise people to sweat only in areas where there are plenty of rivers and streams."

SENTINEL VERDICT:

Smell bad. It's the way forward. And you can forget about unsightly sweat stains because we don't wear clothes.

Dr. Snig's book *Why We're Not Camels* comes out in August. RRP 15.99 pebbles.

NEXT WEEK: ARE HICCUPS A HELP?

A hominid doing some sweating. Unfortunately for his chums it'll be two million years before someone invents the underarm deodorant.

"THEY WERE SMALL AND STUPID!"

NEW GENERATION TRASHES 'SKILLED' BREED

Homo habilis – Yesterday's man.

1,700,000 BC

The latest race of humans has arrived! They're big, they're brainy, they're the best – they're *Homo erectus!*

The new kids on the block take a dim view of their ancestors, *Homo habilis*, whom they brand as "stunted dimwits."

"They may have been clever for their time," said Al 'Upright' Ugg, "but compared to us they're nothing. We're a good 50cm (20in) taller, we're over 20kg (44lbs) heavier and as for our brains – well, let's just say you can think a whole lot better with an extra whole 15% of the gray crinkly stuff."

TOOLS

With their greater size and their advanced tool-making capabilities, *Homo erectus* are certainly making their mark on the evolutionary scene. But some of them are asking the question, 'How come we're so big?'

"Easy," said Al. "Big animals need less energy, relative to their body weight, than small animals. Marmosets, for example, eat proportionally three times as much as a human. So if food is scarce, it's actually more efficient to be big. Still confused? Never mind. You've got plenty of time to figure it out because we're going to be here for the next 1.5 million years!"

5

FIRE IN THE HOLE

Bright Sparks Cause Flame Sensation

450,000 BC

It's hot, it makes you sweat and it's not curry. Yes, it's FIRE!

Previously considered somewhat frightening, the amazing red stuff has become man's best friend. All over the world, humans are using it to cook, to keep warm and to frighten wild beasts.

STRIKES

"There's nothing new about fire," said Norris Nik, President of the Hearth Trust. "You can find it all over the place – bush fires, lightning strikes and volcanoes, for example. But the breakthrough has been introducing it to the home. What you do is make a little pile of stuff, then you find your nearest source of fire, stick a long piece of wood into it and hurry back to light your stuff. If the stuff doesn't burn – and if it's stone or earth it probably won't – try a pile of different stuff. It sounds complicated but it's very simple really."

LOTS

Fire has lots of things going for it, the main one being that it gives us humans more control of our surroundings.

"Before, we depended on the Sun for heat and light," enthused Norris. "Now we can keep warm and dry wherever we are. This not only spells an end to dank caves but it means we can survive in cold places like Europe. And if any Ice Age comes along we can just sit it out."

GROOMING

Scientists aren't sure what fire is, but the current opinion is that it may be some kind of animal.

"In its natural state, fire can be extremely dangerous. However, it is easily tamed and makes a perfect household pet. It's easy to look after, requiring no grooming or vet's visits, and survives happily on a diet of twigs and dry grass. But it does tend to die if given too much to drink.

"Its only drawback is that it leaves nasty stains on the ceiling – but if you have bats already you'll be used to that."

Fire. Once you've tamed it you can't live without it, and it has so many uses. These hungry hominids are using it to confuse and frighten their dinner.

WHAT A DUMP!

Europe a "cultural wasteland"

478,000 BC

Paris in the springtime? Swinging London? Rome, the eternal city? Pah! Give us a break!

Are we disappointed or what? Having trudged all the way to Europe we've found it's got no croissants, no fancy pasta shapes, no cute little cities, no castles and no scandal-prone royal families. In fact, it has a noticeable lack of anything interesting at all.

SHIVER

"It's a cold, miserable place with a lot of mountains, forests and rivers," said shivering Debby Klunk, one of the first wave of settlers. "In the north it's nothing but snow and ice. If we stay here long enough I wouldn't be at all surprised if we ended up with pale skins, an embarrassing amount of body hair and a deplorable sense of rhythm. We should never have left Africa."

BAD

However, sources reveal that Europe isn't as bad as it's made out to be. For starters it's a lot drier than Africa. Moreover, it's got an abundance of animals and is therefore a tip-top destination for hunters.

As numbers grow in the African grasslands and humans begin to feel the pinch we say: "Go North young man!"

LET'S STEPPE ON IT!

MAN GETS INTO THE ASIAN SWING

400,000 BC

"Europe? Why go there?" asks laid-back hominid Hussein Ogg, basking outside his Asian cave. "That's a place for stupid people."

Hussein has a point. Besides being cold and nasty, Europe is also very small. Asia, on the other hand, is mostly warm, is crammed with herds of wildlife, has millions of acres of grassland, and stretches from the Mediterranean to the Pacific.

TOP TRIP

According to a recent hunter-gatherer survey, Asia is our No. 1 destination. Visitors enjoy:
• Nice climate
• Open spaces
• Plenty of food
• The opportunity to become Chinese and invent practically everything before anybody else does.

ENDLESS

Particular attention has been focused on three main rivers – the

Life in a cave, somewhere in Asia. These people could even be heading for China!

Euphrates in Mesopotamia, the Yellow in China and the Indus in India.

"Asia has endless potential," said migration rep. Sally-Sue Grunk. "But it's the big river systems which seem to be the main draw. People say conditions are very comfortable there and given enough time they might even settle down and start farming."

THERE'S NO PLACE LIKE HOME!

By Sentinel correspondent KEN ZOG

Cave shortage prompts hut-building spree

380,000 BC

The world is echoing to the sound of wolf whistles as humans hitch up their furs, dust off their tasteless jokes and get into some serious construction work.

Building has become big business thanks to the pressures of growing populations and an increasing shortage of accommodation.

JUST

"There just aren't enough caves to go round," said Len Mukk (building, decorating and allied trades). "People are coming up and saying, 'Len, knock me up a hut will you? Nothing fancy – just enough space for me and the wife, with somewhere to stick the rest of the family.' So I tell 'em it'll take two weeks and we go from there – strictly pebbles-in-hand, mind you. You can't give credit in today's economic climate."

FLIMSY

Len and his mates are particularly busy in Europe, where decent

"Pah, who did your drains? It'll cost you to have them done properly," say builders.

caves are rare outside of southern France.

"Now and then a customer complains that his home's too flimsy. So I say, 'Look son. You're a hunter-gatherer. You're on the move all the time. You don't want nothing permanent. I've built you a nice little one-room hut out of leafy branches. You've got a row of central posts and some stonework around the edges so's it doesn't blow away. There's a hearth in the middle and space for you all to huddle down in your furs at night. It'll last you the season. Then you'll be moving on. What more do you want? If you're after the Palace of Versailles you should have said so.' There's no reasoning with some, is there?"

HIPPOS IN THE THAMES?

PALM TREES IN GREENLAND?

What's going on?

Where the ice goes when there's an Ice Age. (Just in case you're interested...)

An Investigative Special Report By Olsen Mug*

130,000 BC

Weather! Can't live with it, can't live without it. One millennium you're shivering in your furs, and the next you're squabbling over who gets the suntan lotion first. Hot, cold, hot, cold – it's enough to make you dizzy.

Our unpredictable climate has been a source of irritation for hundreds of thousands of years. But thanks to a special investigation by *Sentinel* super-sleuth, Olsen Mug*, we now know why it acts like it does.

LIES

"The secret lies in the way the Earth goes around the Sun," says Olsen Mug*. "Its orbit isn't always the same. Sometimes it takes us farther away from the Sun, and sometimes it takes us closer.

"This means that we have successive Ice Ages, with glaciers reaching as far south as London and New York, followed by ice-free periods when the earth is warm and fertile, lions wander through Europe, and Britons shelter beneath palm trees, and have to plaster on Factor 20 mud when they sunbathe."

TRAP

"This also explains the puzzling phenomenon of why, at times, land is sometimes above the sea and sometimes beneath it.

When it's cold, most of the world's water is trapped in glaciers and sea levels are low. But when it gets hot, the glaciers melt and we have lots of rain, therefore sea levels rise."

AWKWARD

"Of course, all this tooing and froing does have its awkward moments.

Imagine you're a hippo, wallowing in the Thames.

Then along comes an Ice Age and everybody starts pointing and acting like you don't belong. How embarrassing! And then you have other problems, like not being able to survive because it's too cold, and all the plants you usually eat don't grow where you live anymore. It does make life difficult."

SPELL

How long can we expect this to continue? "Almost indefinitely," says Olsen Mug*. "A prolonged warm spell is predicted from about 13,000 BC, but things will start cooling off around the 21st century AD.

"Maybe by then, however, they'll have discovered the secret of global warming."

IT'S A KNOCKOUT!

100,000 BC

Wise man wins human race

The name's Sap – Hom double sap." Yes, it's hands up to *Homo sapiens sapiens*, the hominid who's licensed to kill.

Despite stiff competition *Hom. sap. sap.* – "the wisest of the wise" – has won through to become the top species on Earth.

"It's all to do with being extremely clever," one *Homo sapiens sapiens* admitted modestly. "With our advanced skills we are in every way superior to any other type of being."

TOOLS

It is all true. *Homo sapiens sapiens* has the most powerful brain of any hominid. And with this massive amount of grey stuff, they have been able to create increasingly complex tools and, above all, develope a sophisticated language. (You can read more about this on pages 24-25, word fans.)

WEIGHT LOSS

It doesn't matter that *Hom. sap. sap.* is only two-thirds the weight of predecessor *Homo erectus*. Being able to speak properly means they can plan, exchange ideas and generally stir things up to their own benefit.

"We may be less bulky than previous species but we have evolved THE definitive brain size," says Dr. Heinrich Zag, an expert in his field. "There will be no comparable brain for the foreseeable future. People in 2000 AD may look back and say, 'Oh how uncivilized they were!' But the fact is, our brains and bodies are exactly the same as those hominids on the 7:30am train from Richmond."

OLSEN MUG
Special Reporter

G'DAY!

CAVEMATES DISCOVER AUSTRALIA!!

Bob Awk and cavemate go in search of Australia's weird and wonderful wildlife.

50,000 BC

First it was Europe, then it was Asia. Now humankind has taken over God's own garden, the land of the roo and the billabong – Australia!

UNDERSIDE

"Strewth, it's peculiar out here, mate," said Bob Awk, one of the first settlers. "The place is hot as a billycan's underside for starters. And the wildlife – well, either someone's playing a joke or they've been left to evolve on their own for too long. Take the kangaroo – big feller, bounds along on its hind legs and carries its kids in a little pouch. Believe me, you don't find that kind of creature anywhere else in the world. Same goes for the wallaby, the koala, the kookaburra and the duck-billed platypus. Queer as a three-dollar bill, the lot of 'em. And as for the XXXXXXX flies…"

"Still, the surfing's good and there's some impressive deserts we can go walkabout in. Could be worse."

GATHER

Australia may be special, but it's not half as special as the way it was colonized. From what our reporters can gather, a huge number of *Homo sapiens sapiens* in Indonesia simply got in their boats and said, "Let's go to Australia." And off they went!

That's pretty amazing, especially when our fortune-tellers predict that it'll be another 51,788 years before anybody else realizes Australia exists.

And, they say, guess what the new bunch of *Hom. sap. saps.* will call the old bunch of *Hom. sap. saps.* when they find them in the 18th century AD? Aborigines! That's from the Latin "*Ab Origine*" which means "From the beginning."

"Well," says Bob, "if we're from the beginning, does that mean they're the end? Future hominids should give that a bit of thought."

"DEAD END" SHOCK
FOR ALTERNATIVES

NEANDERTHALS TOLD "YOU'RE NOBODIES"

40,000 BC

Neanderthals have been doing their best to become an alternative race of humans. But their hopes were quashed at a recent convention of hominids when it was revealed that they lacked all the major qualifications.

DEVASTATED

"I'm devastated!" said beetle-browed Grr Ngg. "We seriously thought we were going places. But as the convention wore on, we realized that we were way behind the competition!"

When the low-slung, chunky Neanderthals first appeared in about 230,000 BC their prospects were as good as anybody else's. True, they looked a bit brutish and ape-like, but they were pretty sophisticated. They cared for their old and sick, they developed a primitive religion and buried their dead with flowers and gifts – though some experts have dismissed this as "mere corpse disposal".

YAK

"It was *"Hom-oh-so-high-and-mighty"* sapiens sapiens who spelled our downfall," said Grr. "We couldn't match his tool-making skills and we simply couldn't understand what he was yakking on about. That was our big failing – speech. *Hom sap sap* can say things like 'Hello gorgeous, how about a date?' All we can do is grunt a bit and make vivid hand signals. We're washed up. By 30,000 BC we won't be here and everyone will say 'Where have those interesting alternative type humans gone?'"

LOST LORE OF THE NEANDERTHALS

No. 1 of our occasional series brings you the secrets of Neanderthal etiquette.

DO THE NEANDER MEANDER!

Your step-by-stumble guide to low-brow deportment.

THINGS TO GET RIGHT

1. Knees bent
2. Chin out
3. Fists curled
4. Brow furrowed

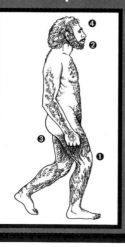

LET'S COME TOGETHER!

GOOD VIBES FOR TRIBES

Being in a big group of fellow hominids is much more fun that mooching around on your own, even if you do end up seeing far more of Uncle Zog than you'd care too.

30,000 BC

It's true – solitary scavenging can damage your health! According to reports you're likely to wither and die unless you're part of a tribe.

Communal living has been the rage for some time now. It started way back when early hominids stood upright and had to care for their children. This led to...

1. Small groups of hominids sticking together.

Then there came the business of hunting which, in order to be successful, required...

2. Cooperation with other groups.

After that came language, and as everyone knows if you speak, you need someone to speak to, so that led to...

3. Gossip, general chit-chat and telling Waffly Zog to shut up on the mammoth hunt.

Then came the pressures of migrating to different places, facing ferocious foreign beasts and checking the toilet for poisonous spiders. This encouraged us to...

4. Group together in the face of adversity in even greater numbers.

And so we formed tribes!

BAND

What's a tribe? Simple. We tend to hunt and gather in groups of 30 or so (12 adults and their kids). When 20 of these groups get together they form a band of around 600. This is a tribe. We meet for big hunts, the odd ceremony and all sorts of other things – like making up new words, exchanging ideas, and most important of all, pairing up and having lots of little hominids.

So, at the end of the day, whether you're in Cairo or Cambridge, you're definitely safer with a tribe!

CAVE DWELLERS IN GRAFFITI UPROAR

"BUT IS IT ART?" SAY CRITICS

15,000 BC

French cave dwellers from Lascaux, in the Dordogne, are hopping mad. They've been branded as "destructive lay-abouts" – all on account of a little wall painting.

"They're vandals," said Lascaux local Mme. Bovary D'Ag. "Before these people moved in, the caves were in excellent condition. Now they're covered in graffiti which will cost a great deal to remove. They call it art. But I've seen them at it. They frolic around, daubing half-finished pictures of animals on the wall and then, late at night, some bright spark'll fill his mouth with paint and spray it out to make an outline of his hand. Frankly, they're a menace."

PLIGHT

"Oh, the plight of the struggling artist!" moaned Vincent van Ugh, a cave painter. "These paintings aren't graffiti. They're the first clear sign of man's artistic ability. They prove we can move beyond the day-to-day business of staying alive and can devote ourselves to more complex activity.

"What's more, art is a vital part of our kids' upbringing. Look. Here's a bull. And here's its hoof print. See? During the long winter months we put a lot of effort into these paintings so that our children can recognize animals and their tracks. It makes the hunting season so much easier. Imagine what would happen if we didn't do it. We'd have kids rushing at a cave lion shouting, "Gazelle! Easy meat!"

A CHILD OF FIVE COULD DO IT

Locals aren't convinced. "Some of the graffiti is quite unrecognizable as man or beast," says Mme. Bovary. "And look at the roof. It's covered in soot. They must have been lighting fires indoors. We don't need these kind of tenants. They're little better than squatters."

The unappreciated cave artists have agreed to move on. But they refuse to remove either the wall paintings or the layers of broken flints and small bones which cover the floor.

"The landlord wants to keep our deposits? Right. There they are, he can keep them!"

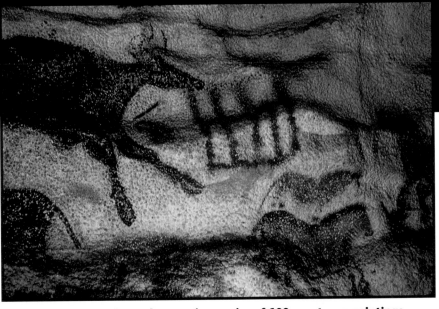

"Cows in French Art". Number one in a series of 100 great cow paintings. Collect the set!

HAND SIGNAL

News has come in that our Stone-Age artists are mostly right-handed. From a sample of 158 hand outlines discovered in the French cave of Gargas, 136 were painted by the right hand and only 22 by the left.

But our art expert warns: "These figures could be misleading. We need to include further data from findings in Germany, Portugal, Italy and Sicily to get a fuller picture of which hand is more commonly used in the European Community."

A report is expected within the next 32,000 years.

THE BUCK

DOESN'T STOP HERE!

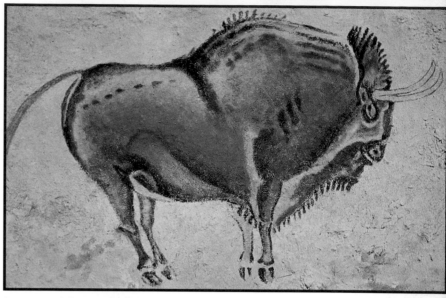

Stone Age joke: Q. What's the difference between a bat and a bison? A. If you don't know I certainly won't be asking you to go hunting! (Cue polite laughter.)

LAND OF OPPORTUNITY BECKONS

12,000 BC

It's a whole new continent! Intrepid trekkers in northern Siberia have discovered a land bridge leading from the Eurasian continent to America!

UNPLEASANT

Early reports say America is a cold and unpleasant place with little going for it.

"You'd have to be an Eskimo to survive there," said one disappointed colonist. "It's like living in Alaska."

Land bridge to Alaska

They went thataway!

However, geographical experts have pointed out that the place they've found is, in fact, Alaska, and that a sunnier climate awaits to the south.

Sentinel reporters have followed emigrants on their great trek, and can confirm that America gets hotter the farther down you go.

PASS

"First you pass through this cold area," says cub-reporter Jimmy Olsen-Clod, "Then you reach a country of big open spaces and endless opportunity. It's a fantastic place. There's endless prairies with million-strong herds of bison, and fields and fields of things like beans and corn."

"These foods are brand-new to us. But then so are a lot of other things here – turkeys, avocados, guinea-pigs, squashes and an irritating little dog called a Chihuahua."

Jimmy Olsen-Clod predicts that it'll take at least 2,000 years to reach the bottom of the continent.

"There's so much to see and explore. I reckon we won't be in Chile until 10,000 BC at the earliest."

WE'RE GOING TO POT

"Not a copy," say Japanese

"It's all our own work," insist Japanese potters.

12,000 BC

Japan has invented the most useful piece of pottery to date – the pot.

"It is a major breakthrough," said Professor Tanaka Stig. "We are now able to construct containers of any type we like simply by shaping lumps of clay and baking them in a covered pit."

"Unfortunately we are not able to use these pots as much as we would like. They are, alas, too heavy and too fragile to fit in with our hunting and gathering existence. Never-the-less, the art of pottery is here to stay and will undoubtedly be useful if people settle down to become farmers."

CLAIM

Opponents are already claiming the invention is a mere copy, and point to the existence of pottery skills in Czechoslovakia as far back as 25,000 BC.

LACKING

However, Professor Stig haughtily dismisses the earlier examples of pottery as "mere statuettes" which are "utterly lacking in usefulness."

"Pottery is a genuine first for Japan," he insists "and should fill us with justifiable national pride."

12

MAMMOTH SHORTAGE

CAUSES CONCERN

LIFESTYLE COLLAPSE
PREDICTED FOR MANY

12,000 BC

Residents of eastern Europe and northern Asia are in big trouble. The mammoth, their main source of food, is disappearing FAST.

The mammoth has been a big item for centuries. Hunters have valued it for its legendary size (*Ed. actually, it's slightly smaller than an elephant*), its ivory tusks, its wonderful woolly hide and equally woolly brain.

Mammoths are so stupid and cumbersome that people have had no trouble laying an ambush and picking them off as they plod through the countryside. Sometimes they didn't even have to kill them. Quite often they found dead ones deep frozen and covered in ice and snow. All they had to do then was thaw them out at leisure using the miracle of fire.

SHREW

But all that's in the past. Nowadays, hunters lying in wait on the mammoth trail count themselves lucky if they bag a pygmy shrew.

What's happened? Mrs. Dunk, from the Russian village of Kostienki, tells all: "It's the men! They wouldn't stop killing mammoths. I told them they'd have problems if they carried on, but they took no notice. Now look what's happened. We've run out of the things. What can I do? Mr. Dunk won't touch his tea unless there's a big chunk of mammoth on the plate."

HALF

Experts say Mrs. Dunk is half right. The climate around Kostienki is also changing. It used to be freezing cold, and now it's getting warmer. And as the snow and ice retreats to the north, so the few remaining mammoths are following after it.

"Yes," bellowed a mammoth spokesperson, "we've all got these thick shaggy coats, so we like things nice and cold. This hot weather makes us all sweaty and bad tempered, so we're following our chums the reindeer to colder climes, where we can bask around in snow drifts."

This is very bad news for Kostienki, which has taken mammoth-mania to the limits. Not only do its inhabitants eat mammoths but they even build houses out of them. The doors are made of tusks and the walls are made of various other bones. The whole thing is pinned together with smaller bones, tied up with mammoth sinew and covered with hide.

Bone sweet bone – it's a mammoth house.

The framework alone of a typical mammoth-house, 5m (16ft) wide, weighs a staggering 21,000kg (46,000lb)! And some of their houses are much bigger than that!

THERE'S MORE

And what do you do in Kostienki when it's a bit cold? You throw a few mammoth bones on the fire! What do you do if you feel like creating a figurine of old Mrs. Zunk with her big nose? You get out your knife and a chunk of mammoth tusk!

MAD

Tools, toys, houses, food, clothes, furniture, knick-knacks – they're mammoth mad. In the whole village there's hardly a spoon or a needle that didn't start life as part of a mammoth.

So what are the Kostienkians going to do now?

"It's a clear choice," said Mr. Dunk. "We either make do with something else or go north in search of any remaining mammoths."

Bye-bye mammoth, we're missing you already!

Experts say overhunting, a changing environment and having a small brain has finished off the mammoth.

MAMMOTH UPDATE NEXT WEEK

FARMING FRENZY

HITS FERTILE CRESCENT

HUNTER GATHERERS WARN OF "MUTANT INVASION"

Some new-fangled farmers buckle down to some reaping what they sow, counting their chickens, and not letting one bad apple spoil the whole barrel.

7,500 BC

I t's put-your-feet-up time in the Middle East, as folk discover the delights of farming.

Lifestyle experts from the Fertile Crescent ("It's a big lump of land running from Egypt to Iran, including the bottom bit of Turkey," says our Geography Correspondent) have found that folk live much more comfortably if they stop hunting and gathering, and take up farming instead.

SEED

What is farming? We asked a local agrispokesman: "It's simple. You throw a few handfuls of seed around and wait for it to grow. Then you eat whatever it grows into. In between times you wander about waving a big stick, shouting, "Get off my land!" It's more exciting than picking berries and it's a whole lot easier than chasing antelopes, I can tell you!"

But hunter-gatherers are lobbying for agriculture to be outlawed. "It's a menace to the natural order and it's putting us out of business," said a representative. "Farmers are selecting mutant plants which grow bigger than normal. And then they're planting them! It ought to be banned NOW!"

DESTROY

Farmers have laughed off suggestions that agriculture will destroy the countryside. "In the Fertile Crescent we're growing wheat, barley, peas, lentils – the works. It's the up-and-coming thing. India, China and South America will all be at it soon. And I'll tell you why. 15 square km (5.82 square miles) of fields can support 150 farmers. It takes 650 square km (250 square miles) to support 25 hunter-gatherers. Need I say more?"

STAINS

In a further break from tradition, farmers are building villages. These groups of dwellings are made from wood and stone, are usually found near a spring, and are designed to last for several years. Opponents say that villages are only the start and will lead to mega-settlements with inner-city crime and graffiti-stained underpasses.

Hunter-gatherers are planning a "Hunt 'n Gather" protest march to draw attention to this unpleasant prospect. Their precise route is unknown but they are expected to wander in small, unhappy groups across Africa, Europe and Asia.

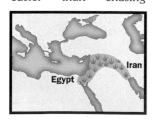

It's fertile and it's a crescent.

14

A STITCH IN TIME...

FUR FLIES AS FLAX SPARKS CLOTHING CRAZE

7,500 BC

I t's official! Those Kill-things-and-wear-'em days are over. From now on it's pelts off and clothes on as the rag trade takes over!

Thanks to an enterprising bunch of farmers, we no longer have to wear furs. Instead we can wear "cloth". This miracle fabric is guaranteed to be light, comfortable, quickly mended and easily replaced.

FLAX FAX

Sentinel reporters have identified the source of "cloth" as a plant called flax. According to informants, raw flax has to be soaked, pounded vigorously and then rubbed on the thigh to make a weavable strand.

"It's hard work," agreed style guru Giovanni Lugg, "But it's worth the trouble. As for furs, they're completely out of fashion – unless you live somewhere really cold. All that hair, and those rubbery fleshy tendrils. Ugh! Take it from me. Cloth's the people's choice."

Fashionable flax takes hours of dedicated work to process into the new miracle material "cloth".

TAME THAT BEAST

DOMESTICATION SENSATION!

Farming isn't just about crops. You'll need tame animals too. Here at the *Sentinel* we've drawn up a handy guide to a happy barnyard. Follow our chart to what stings and bites and what doesn't (or oughtn't to, at any rate) and you'll never go hunting or gathering again.

Aurochs

Stands 1.8m (6ft) at the shoulder. Muscly and bad-tempered. Has big, curved horns. Dislikes red rags. Provides a great deal of meat, leather and milk. Bellows and goes "Moo".

VERDICT – *An unlikely candidate, but since it provides so much, it's worth the trouble. Capture a few, breed from the placid ones and Hey Presto! you've got cows.*

Snake

Comes in all sizes. Slithery. Often poisonous. Impossible to milk. Unreliable egg-layer. Goes "Hiss".

VERDICT – *Don't bother. But keep a few on the refuse tip because they eat rats.*

Sheep and goat

About knee-height. Has horns. Provides warm, thick wool, milk and meat. Goes "Baa" and "Mehh".

VERDICT – *Ideal for the farm. They're herd animals, so once you've caught a few young 'uns they'll think you're herd leader and will do what you tell 'em (sort of).*

Wild boar

Smaller than sheep. Fat. Bristly. Has tusks and twirly tail. Provides bacon, chops and crackling. Goes "Oink".

VERDICT – *Yummy! Every home should have one. Is intelligent and eats anything, so is a natural for those rundown filth-strewn farms. Needs almost no taming. Comes home at night of its own accord. Often called Pig.*

Cat

Small. Plain, striped or tabby. Edible only on TV documentaries about funny foreigners. Goes "Miaouw" and "Browwp". Can scratch when irritated.

VERDICT – *Will accept domestication with a superior shrug. Eats mice, rats, small rabbits and birds and leaves their indigestible parts on your floor. Tends to trip you up but can be kicked very satisfactorily. Likes scratching furniture which is OK so long as your sitting log doesn't evolve into a sofa which you've upholstered at great expense. Comforting lap accessory.*

Believe it or not, over time this thing can be bred into a French poodle! (Would we lie to you?!?)

Tiger

Large, striped, frightening thing. Big teeth. Big appetite. Prone to scenes of explicit violence. Goes "Wraaaaaaagh."

VERDICT – *Only worth keeping if you have a particularly irksome milkman or if you belong to the "I-think-pit-bulls-and-Dobermans-are-soft" school of pet lovers. Otherwise forget it. Try its lesser cousin, the cat.*

Fly

Has wings. Small and black. Plenty of eggs but too small to see. Creepy eyes. Spits on food. Tastes through feet. Goes "Buzz".

VERDICT – *Impossible to domesticate. Avoid like the plague.*

Wolf

Small, rangy scavenger. Howls at night. Not worth eating but plays educational role in bedtime stories. Goes "Woof".

VERDICT – *A pack animal, so if you get a puppy it'll follow you around. Will help you out hunting, will fetch your slippers when you come home and will bark all day if you leave it inside.*

WARNING

Take care not to breed from animals that are too closely related, otherwise THIS could happen, or worse!

AGRICULTURE
OR AGRI-VATION?

6,500 BC

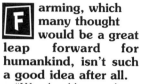

Farming, which many thought would be a great leap forward for humankind, isn't such a good idea after all.

"We should never have given up hunting and gathering," says farmer Giles Gnug from Jericho, in the Fertile Crescent. "Agriculture is hard work, the diet's less varied, bandits keep stealing our food and we catch all these nasty new diseases."

GERMS

Diseases? Yes. If you live close to animals for too long, you catch viruses from them. The result is that human beings, who've never had a cold in their lives, are now prone to all sorts of deadly things like measles, smallpox and influenza.

"And that's not all," says farmer Giles. "If you live in a village, as most farmers do, surrounded by lots of people and all their filth, that means you're much likelier to catch whatever's going around than if you're hunting and gathering on the plains.

"Dysentery, typhoid, tuberculosis – you name it, we've got it. And some of these villages are in really unhealthy places. I've heard of this farming community at Çatal Hüyük in Turkey, for example, which is surrounded by mosquito-infested marshes and everyone catches malaria and dies at an early age. But then it was one of the first settlements, so maybe they didn't know any better."

In fact, most farmers can expect to die before they're 35 – or 30 if they're women.

So why do people do it? "Ah well," says Giles. "The trouble is there's so many of us. Once we started to get a regular supply of food we bred like rabbits, and now we're stuck with it. If we went back to hunting and gathering we'd all starve. It's too late to change now."

Sheep. They may look cute and cuddly, but beneath the thin veneer of baaahsome amiability there lies a deadly, malevolent menace to mankind.

HOW IRRIGATING

Water load of old ditches!

3,500 BC

Wouldn't it be nice if we could grow more crops? Well now we can – thanks to irrigation, a cunning method of bringing water to places that are otherwise as dry as a desert.

Everyone knows that a bit of water helps crops grow, and that river mud is tip-top stuff for growing things in. But what do you do if you've got water in some places and not in others? Simple. You dig a ditch so that water flows from the watery places to the non-watery places. This way you'll turn a barren wasteland into a moist, silt-filled paradise where wheat waves golden in the breeze.

COMPLAINTS

Huge harvests have been recorded in countries such as Mesopotamia and Egypt where irrigation is commonplace.

But the people who dig the ditches are not happy with their lot.

"It's hard work," said one field hand. "We not only have to build these ditches but we have to maintain them. You've got to clear away the silt, you've got to make sure the water runs where you want it to, and then you've got to farm the fields. And then you've probably got to dig more ditches because some bright spark has decided to irrigate the entire Arabian desert."

MASSIVE

The widespread fear is that irrigation is too difficult for farmers to do on their own, and that it will give rise to a massive workforce paid by a single, all powerful government.

"This means we'll end up with kings and stuff. They'll demand taxes to pay the workers and this will lead to a lot of hard work for us peasants," said a peasant.

DID YOU KNOW...

- **Nothing grows in the Sahara because all the goodness has been washed out of the soil by massive amounts of rainfall.**

- **The hefty old Aurochs – giant ancestor of the cow – won't be extinct until AD 1671.**

- **A typical Stone-Age head of corn is only the size of a thumb nail! (This is why we haven't bothered inventing pointy things to stick in the ends of corn-on-the-cob!)**

Lost for smalltalk? Read The Sentinel!

TRANSPORT SPECIAL

"YOU KNOW YOU'RE GOING PLACES WITH THE SENTINEL!"

WHEEL MEET AGAIN

The Shape Of The Future

3,000 BC

It's round, it's made of wood, and it's the greatest scientific breakthrough since the sharp stone. Yes, it's the WHEEL!

Humans are on the road at last, and the world is rumbling to the sound of traffic as we go wheel crazy.

A potter at a wheel. Would you believe this is the first step toward the Ferrari Testarossa?

POTS

According to our reporters, the wheel was first invented by potters, who needed a round, flat thing that they could spin a lump of muddy clay on to make pot-making easier. Then one smarty-pants said, "Hey! Why not turn a couple of these on their sides, attach them to a cart, and see what happens!"

Well, the rest is history.

CANS

Nowadays, anybody who's even vaguely with-it has a set of wheels. Teenager Suzie Zagg says: "They're so cool! Because they go merrily round and round rather than drag unpleasantly along the ground, you can go places faster, and carry heavier weights than ever before!"

NUTS

Opponents are already dismissing the miracle invention as "merely an altered square." They say that although wheels allow people to move things more easily, they do have a big disadvantage: **they need a smoothish surface to travel over.**

Given that a lot of our terrain is made up of rocks, ravines, steep hills and impenetrable woodland, it'll be a while before the wheel reaches its full potential.

BREATH

"Wheels are OK, but I'm not holding my breath," says mule-driver Abdullah Zupp. "In the future, whenever there's a major civilization, somebody will build roads and things will be hunky-dory.

"But when those civilizations collapse, the first thing to go is the roads... well, no roads, no wheels. Believe me, this new technology's all very clever, but the smart money's staying with pack animals."

SETTLE DOWN, SETTLE DOWN

A city. Citizens will have to wait around 5,000 years before they can complain about how bad the buses are.

LIFE IS HOTTER IN SUMER!

3,000 BC

It's all change in Sumer, the Fertile Crescent's most up-and-coming region. The world's first city, Uruk, has become the biggest draw since cave painting.

"It's like a village, but much, much bigger," says reporter H. P. Sos. "The authorities saw how people were settling down and forming communities wherever there was enough land and water to support farming. So they decided to go one step farther. Result: the city."

Uruk really is something different. Not only is it bigger than a village but the way it's run is entirely new. It's ruled

Here's Uruk!

by a single king who organizes citizens to dig irrigation canals, collect farm produce, police the streets and, above all, pay him taxes.

There's a big temple in the middle of the city, which is dedicated to a god. Everybody is expected to supply the god with offerings of grain.

The king takes this grain and uses it to pay people to dig more canals, collect more farm produce, police more streets and collect more taxes so he can pay other people to defend the city, build walls around it, erect a bigger temple, and bully the previous people into digging more canals, producing more grain and paying more taxes. (Got that straight?)

HARD

But Uruk isn't only about hardship. It's also about TRADE! The city contains lots of non-farming citizens who make their living by supplying farmers with things they don't have time to make for themselves – chairs, tables, beds, pots, jewels, garden gnomes and so on.

LONG

What this means is that, so long as you've got the grain coming in, a city will support as many trades as there is demand for them. This, in turn, means that someone can survive without farming themselves.

"Cities are the hot-bed of invention," says H. P. Sos. "I predict Uruk's example will be followed across Asia, from India to China. Once you start building these things, there's no turning back."

WRITE ON!

Clay Tablets Get Full Marks

3,000 BC

Speaking is old hat, according to citizens in Mesopotamia. They've come up with a revolutionary method of communication which involves scratching symbols on clay tablets. Enthusiasts have already given it a name – WRITING!

"Writing's very easy," said Bart Jugg, a scribe. "All you have to do is draw a picture of the thing you want to describe. If you want to say you've got ten goats, you draw ten pictures of a goat. If you want to talk about the Sun, you draw something round with a few lines sticking out."

"After a little practice, you don't have to draw an actual goat. Instead you can do a shorthand squiggle and everybody will recognize it as 'goat'. You can also use symbols for less obvious things. Day and night, for example. What do they look like? Easy – a sun for day and a moon for night. Some symbols are less obvious – such as an arrow, which is our sign for life. But honestly, so long as everybody knows what each symbol means it doesn't matter what they look like. You could draw an

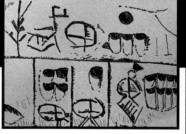

Is it a squiggle, or is it a WORD?

elephant as the sign for a teaspoon and that would be fine."

Royal employees are the people most likely to benefit from writing. Temple scribes will particularly welcome the development as they have to record every bit of tax paid by every man or woman in the region.

NEW THREAT TO STONE

2,500 BC

Reports are coming in of a brand new alloy called bronze. (Science fans will know that an alloy is a mixture of metals.) Developed in South-east Asia, bronze is a mixture of copper and tin. Manufacturers are hailing it as the hardest metal yet made. They have already issued a limited number of bronze weapons and expect to produce tailor-made bronze body-protection shortly.

BRONZED OFF

Supporters say the alloy marks a new era – the Bronze Age. Opponents maintain stone is still best. "If you want to avoid an arrow you don't need metal. All you have to do is duck behind the nearest rock."

The debate continues.

Metalwork – it's a dirty job, but someone's got to do it.

FOR SALE

Square piece of wood. Could be a wheel if given the chance. Full Service History. One lady owner. TK/105

Sharp stick. Unwanted present. Good for prodding. Would suit elderly grouch. TK/23

Mastodon jaw. Yes, I have one. Ideal hand weapon. Hardly used. 10 pebbles. No offers. TK/801

Skins. Skins. Skins. Every fur from mouse to mammoth. Dirt cheap. Fell off the back of an animal. TK/224

IMPORTANT NOTICE

Due to unforeseen circumstances of an underground nature EILAT MINES is pleased to announce the following vacancies:

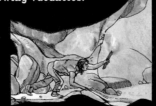

- 2 Hewers • 4 Diggers
- 2 Haulers • 2 Hackers
- 3 Coughers
- 4 Splutterers
- 5 Cursers-and-Spitters
Also 1 Superintendent

Seam-face workers must possess all the usual copper-mining skills. Please note that Eilat Mines operates a narrow-gallery policy therefore children and unusually small adults will be given preference over full-size applicants.
The post of Superintendent is open to responsible overseers with a proven track record. The successful candidate will be expected to provide his/her own easy chair and magazines.

APPLY WITH FULL DETAILS IN THE FIRST INSTANCE TO: THE BOSS, COPPER HOUSE, EILAT, NR. THE GULF OF AQABA, FERTILE CRESCENT.

THE EDITOR SPEAKS

The Get Ahead Sentinel – You Know It Makes Sense

Well, the Stone Age is over at last. ABOUT TIME TOO! Stone is SO unglamorous. If you want to get ahead in the world you're not going to do it by chipping away at lumps of flint. It's OK if you're starting out. But let's face it. It's not the kind of technology that's going to get us to the Moon, IS IT?

HUNTING AND GATHERING

It kept us fit, provided a varied diet and allowed us to exist in a natural state alongside the rest of the animal kingdom. But all good things come to an end. And when you think about it, it did keep population levels very low. If we'd stuck at it most of us wouldn't be here. Since the *SENTINEL* always puts its readers first, we say that's bad news. THE MORE OF YOU THE BETTER!!!

FIRE

Wasn't that a breakthrough? We think it'll provide the world's energy needs, in one form or another, for thousands and thousands of years. In fact, we vote it the NUMBER ONE discovery of the Stone Age!!!

MAMMOTHS

Farewell, big woolly friends. You were great while you lasted, and we shall miss your fearsome bellow. But as they say in Çatal Hüyük – this place ain't big enough for the both of us.

EVOLUTION

Whaddya reckon? WE don't think we need it any more. After all, you only evolve in order to adapt to new environments. But since we can pretty well control our environment we don't need to adapt any more. How about THAT?!!! But there's a long way to go yet. Who knows, if they ever invent computer keyboards we might have to evolve 26 fingers. LET'S WAIT AND SEE!

CITIES

We love 'em. Lots of buzz, lots of new ideas, lots of jobs, lots of wealthy people = lots more people reading the *SENTINEL!* THAT'S PROGRESS FOR YOU!!!

SHORT SHARP SHOCK SENTINEL WEAPONS

INSTRUMENTS OF DEATH

"Sticks and stones may break my bones but words will never hurt me." Anyone told they have a face like a baboon's bottom may quibble, but who could deny that sticks and stones do break bones with alarming efficiency.

Experts say that weapons are here to stay. So whether you want to kill a chicken or an attacking nomad, the choice is clear. If you're not armed you're extinct. It's that simple.

In a special reader's service, our weapons correspondent Roy Zogg answers your killing queries.

Chomp

Dear Roy,

We're a fairly harmless bunch when you look at us. We've got dainty little fingers instead of sharp claws, and our teeth can just about chew an apple, rather than bite the head off our prey with a single chomp. We're obviously meant to be plant munching, cuddly little creatures who like cooing at butterflies and hugging trees. So how come we're waving weapons around like there's no tomorrow?

Larry Zugg, 42 Sabre-Tooth Avenue, Hutsville

Having dainty fingers means you can make things with them. You don't see lions lashing together bows and arrows with their big nasty paws do you? Your hand on its own can't do much as a weapon, but pick up a rock or a sharp stick and you're in business!

Two good reasons for making weapons:
One. Try defending yourself against a pan-ther without one.
Two. If you want to eat something more interesting than berries and seeds, chances are you'll have to catch it. True, you could hang around until you come across a half-eaten gazelle, but why wait, when you can KILL IT YOURSELF!

Ferocious

Dear Roy,

This hunting is a frightening business, even if you have got a sharp stick or a flint axe! My chum Joe Gorr says it's best to hunt the biggest animals like mammoths, but I think this is too dangerous, and we should stick to killing a few dormice every now and then.

Bob Stigg, 14a Cave Crescent, Tarrpitts

Aaaaah, the great big or small debate. Face facts, Mr. Stigg, kill a mammoth and you can keep your family fed for a month. Kill a dormouse, and you're squabbling over who gets what for breakfast, and you can forget about lunch and tea. I know mammoths can look pretty ferocious, but take it from me they're worth the extra effort.

Worms

Dear Roy,

I'm a pretty eager hunter, with plenty of raw courage, but I'm not having much luck. Whenever I try and kill a mammoth it runs away before I can get near it.

Jack Grok, "Dungatherin", Fossil

What you need, Mr. Grok, is TEAMWORK. Get together a bunch of pals armed with club and spears. No bows an arrows, or slingshot you've got to get right u close to down a man moth. (Tell them to ge to your cave at sunris too, – the early ma catcheth the mammoth.

All huddle together i a circle. Then you say "OK guys, what are u gonna do?" and they a shout, "Kill a man moth!" Then you a march off into the plai going "Whoop whoop "Yeeeahhh", and stu like that. All the nois will rouse a sleepin

LETTER OF THE WEEK

Muuuuurdah

Dear Roy,

We all know that weapons are very good for hunting, but guess what I heard yesterday – you can even kill people with them! Quite a shock that.

Harold Jodd, A hole in the ground, Clubland

Yes, Mr. Jodd, it's quite the latest thing. We've had weapons for ages, but until quite recently we've just used them to hunt. (Although, to be frank, there has been the odd argument over a mate or a gazelle that spilled over into a murder.)

Lately, what with fertile land getting a little scarcer now there's more of us humans around, and some of us settling down in farms and towns while others roam around, some bright sparks have realized you can kill your way to wealth and prosperity rather than work hard at it!

This is called warfare, and it basically involves all the skills we've learned from hunting – same weapons, same cooperating in groups – only the people that do it are called soldiers.

BASHEM & RUNN

FOR ALL YOUR SLAUGHTERING NEEDS

Still going clubbing? You're obsolete! Catch up on all the latest hi-tech weaponry, including the phenomenal no-bodily-contact bow and arrow, at a settlement showroom near you NOW!

The classics

Flint hand axe

For those on a tight budget. Simply grab and stab. What could be easier! 1 pebble

Stick

Another budget special, and still as useful as ever. Sharpen with flint hand axe for added effectiveness. 1 pebble

The best of the beast

Antelope bone

More wallop for your pebbles than any other thigh bone available! 3 pebbles

Antelope horn

The perfect dagger, for those right-up-close encounters. Still only 4 pebbles

Tooled-up

Bola

Swing around the head and throw. You don't see baboons doing this! Ideal for those small to middle-sized prey. 7 pebbles

Spear

Fire-hardened tip for penetration power where you really need it. Buy of the week. Only 5 pebbles!

Deluxe spear

With hand-lashed flint tip. Will pierce even the toughest hide. 8 pebbles

Deluxe axe

Try our new-improved deluxe axe, too. Stone top with added handle, gives you extra zing in your swing! 10 pebbles

The very latest

Spear thrower

More power to your shoulder! Improves spear range by up to 50%. Simply lob and collect. A hit every time! 7 pebbles

Sword

Think of it as a super dagger. It's longer, so you can stab from a safe distance. Available in copper and bronze. 10-15 pebbles

Bow and arrow

The ultimate in warfare safety. Lightweight and portable. Long range (Up to 50m (160ft)). Fast – your arrows fly swifter than a swooping hawk. Arrow projectile effective on all prey up to size of antelope and humans. 10 pebbles

BASHEM AND RUNN - SLAUGHTERING SINCE 240,000BC

MRS. OGG'S STONE AGE BEAUTY PAGE

Put the stunningly sensational back into the Stone Age, with the Fashion and Beauty column you can't afford to miss!

MRS. OGG — VOTED TOP STYLE COLUMNIST OF THE ERA BY READERS OF CAVEWEAR WEEKLY

SO WHAT'S HAPPENING IN YOUR CAVE?

BEAUTY AT ITS MOST BASIC

SWAGGER

• Readers out to trap a mate will be interested to know that body painting is IN. Red clay is plentiful enough, and washes off with a simple application of water.

Other adornments to put a swagger in your stagger include ambergris perfume (this comes from whale intestines, and smells far nicer than you'd think) and spruce tree leaf resin to sweeten the breath.

You can't go wrong with a few feathers too, draped in your hair or clothing.

BEADY

• Even though they're such hard work to make, beads will always be fashionable. I know it can take up to three hours to make a single polished bead from a sliver of mammoth tusk. But once it's done, it'll stay like that forever.

A charming necklace adds allure to any outfit.

You can make beads from animal teeth, seashells, soapstone, and even pebbles. When you've got a good number, string them together to make a necklace, or sew them onto clothing, using a bone needle and some wool thread.

Then you'll have something of beauty that can be passed on through the generations, and treasured by your descendants for all eternity!

HAIR WEAR NEWS

• Try braiding. This means weaving three strands into one. Not only does it keep you out of mischief, it's the perfect antidote to boring, long straight hair.

Shells make a pretty dress sensational!

FREE FACT SLAB
on clothes dyes available now!

NEXT WEEK: MAKE YOUR OWN BONE BROOCH

FASHION TIPS

What's all the rage with the new style "clothes"?

FUR ENOUGH

Natural materials are this season's hottest body covering, and fur is still the number one choice for Stone Age trend-setters.

It's warm, it's easy on the eye, and it doesn't take too many brain cells to realize how to wear it. It's not perfect of course – it stinks like an old goat (especially if it IS an old goat) and it gets soggy when it rains. Still, if you want style and sophistication, you've got to pay the price!

LEATHER OR NOT

Catching up in popularity is the fabric of the future – leather. It's like fur but without the hair (you have to scrape this off.) Leather takes a while to prepare before you wear it. It has to be "tanned" (coated in a liquid called tannin to preserve it), then pulled tight across a frame to stretch it.

Leather can be cut into any shape, which means you can get it to fit as snugly as you like. You can also dye it pretty shades, or cut patterns in it.

It's extremely hard-wearing, and really keeps out the wind and the rain.

WOOL REALLY

Readers who like to peer at the very outer rim of the cutting edge of fashion technology will be curious about another new fabric. It's called wool, and it comes from those docile and bleating creatures, sheep. You can pluck it off the sheep as it sheds its coat, but don't wear it just as it is, it'll only blow off.

What you need to do is twist the wool around a wooden spindle to make a thin thread. Then you take the thread and weave it carefully together in a loom. Its very warm and versatile!

A loom. You can make socks with this!

HAVE AN ICE DAY

THERE'S NO BUSINESS LIKE SNOW BUSINESS SAYS TOP INUIT

8,000 BC

We humans have spread to almost every inhospitable corner of the world. From the howling wastes of Siberia to the baking plains of Arizona, we're there! But how do you make a living in a land where much of the sea is frozen solid and almost the only natural resources are seals and whales and ice and snow?

It's a piece of cake, says top Inuit Barry Yagg of the Arctic circle. You just have to make do with the little bit of everything that's actually available. Find out how he does it with the *Sentinel*'s roving reporter Don Stigg.

Don Stigg. So what do you eat out there? I bet you get sick of seafood!

Barry Yagg. During the summer we get to eat reindeer and deer. It's winter that's mainly seafood – seal, walrus, fish – but also the odd polar bear if we can catch one. Incidentally, if you ever do catch a polar bear, don't eat the liver. It's so poisonous it'll kill you.

DS. You'll need something a bit more substantial than a hook and line to catch a seal!

BY. Too true. Sometimes we use kayak canoes and hunt with harpoons. Our kayaks are made entirely from animals – bone frame and skin covering, treated with a waterproof glue made from boiling up various animal bits and pieces.

The other way we catch sea life is by digging holes in the ice. Seals pop up in them from time to time for a breath of air, and we nab them then. (We learned this trick from our arch enemy the polar bear.)

DS. So what does the fashionable Inuit wear for a day out?

BY. From the top of our one-piece tunic and hood, to the tip of our waterproof socks and boots, all our clothes are made from animals. They're mainly the leathery hides of seals and walruses, and fur from foxes and hares. These materials keep

Rudolph Reindeer's red nose would never again guide Santa through a foggy Christmas Eve.

their natural owners nice and snug, and do the trick for us too.

We like our clothes to be airtight but loose, so there's a layer of air to warm up next to our skin. We use bone needles and animal guts to sew the clothes together.

DS. Is it really true you live in ice houses?

BY. Sometimes... In the summer we're no different from everyone else. We make little huts from animal hides wrapped around a bone frame.

In the winter we also make shelters called igloos, from blocks of ice coated with snow. We have a little ice window at the top too. They make surprisingly warm little dens.

DS. There's so little wood around, what do you do for fuel?

BY. Any wood we find we use for weapons.

Fortunately, our animals come to the rescue once again. The sea mammals here, such as seals and whales, are covered in a layer of thick fat called blubber, which keeps out the cold. Blubber burns very well, so we heat food with it. We also brighten up our igloos with little blubber-burning lamps!

DS. It all sounds ingenious! But honestly, why would anyone want to live somewhere where it's so freezing cold?

BY. If your idea of heaven is a beach in Majorca, then it's obviously not for you. But we like it out here – it's not too crowded, we don't have tribes of passing nomads burning our villages and stealing our corn, and if it's always cold, you soon stop complaining about it because you've never known anything else!

NEXT WEEK: SOME LIKE IT HOT — MEET THE DESERT DWELLERS!

YOU WHAT???

Get with the new-style speech in the Sentinel column that TELLS IT LIKE IT IS!

10 THINGS YOU NEVER KNEW ABOUT TALKING

1 Experts think that we hominids have been able to talk since *Homo habilis* in 2,000,000 BC, who could say a few basic words like *"food"*, *"drink"* and *"do you come here often"*.

2 *Homo erectus* polished up his grammar and vocabulary a bit, and was able to string together the odd sentence. "*Not... woolly... mammoth... again. Me... want... smoked... salmon.*"

3 Only *Homo Sapiens* has been able to talk properly, as our mouths and throats are the right shape for rapid, sophisticated conversation. "*If I see you wearing that filthy animal skin one more time, I'm going to throw it in the fire. D'you hear? And don't look at me like that when I'm talking to you.*"

4 Humans are not the only creatures that talk to each other. Lots of animals grunt and squawk to communicate. Some insects even exchange smells to tell each other what they think. (Don't go getting any ideas...)

5 Some animals even have a small vocabulary. The Vervet monkey has about 10 different grunts and eeks, including one for eagle and one for cheetah.

6 Humans on the other hand have THOUSANDS OF WORDS for things, and can string these words together to explain complex new ideas, teach old dogs new tricks, and let other people know exactly how they feel. (Pretty bad! Top of the world! etc, etc.)

7 These words can also describe things other people have not seen, anticipate events in the future and recall events in the past. Try doing that with a few grunts and barks.

"Errr, me think it a wolf!!!" The game of Charades swiftly follows the invention of speech.

8 To make words your tongue goes to 50 different positions in your mouth.

9 Speech experts think it was the need to gather food together and cooperate to stay alive, that led us to develop our complex languages.

10 Although words for the same thing are different all over the world, what is similar about all human speech are the basic rules of grammar. (This means the way words are arranged.)

IT'S A... CAVE

There's a word for everything these days. Tree, river, mammoth – you name it, we've got it! But where <u>do</u> words come from? Language eggheads have thought about this, and come up with several theories. Here at the *SENTINEL* we cast a critical eye on what they're saying...

EXPERTS SAY	THE SENTINEL SAYS
Words began as imitations of natural sounds.	Works OK for Whooosh, Splash, Burp, Woof and Meow. But how do you explain Prehistoric, Cave painting, Knife and fork... the list is endless.
Words began as utterances along with emotional reactions.	Works OK for Aaaaaagh, Bleurrrrrgh and Waaaaagh, but try writing a poem with those!
Words were prompted by facial accompaniments to gestures we made to one another.	Call us crabby old cynics, but apart from a lip-smacking "Yum Yum", we can't think of anything else that fits this description.

COMMENT

THE SENTINEL SAYS

It looks like language is quite a mystery. But wherever words come from, one thing's for sure – everyone in your tribe has to use the same words to mean the same thing. After all, it's no good saying "Go and play hide and seek with a sabre-toothed tiger", if what you really mean is "Your High and Mightiness, I would be most delighted to marry your daughter."

GET STUFFED

WHAT'S COOKING?

with the Sentinel's cookery correspondent Pierre de Zoque

What's cooking, *mes amis*? Cooking is when you heat something up before you eat it!

Yes, you lazy bones, I know it takes more effort, but not only does cooked food taste, look and smell nicer, it's easier to digest and much better for you. (Nutritionists among you will be interested to know that this is because heating food makes it easier for humans to digest proteins and carbohydrates in it.)

We all know the story about the piece of mammoth meat that fell on the fire and tasted much nicer after it had sizzled a bit, but just throwing meat on a fire isn't exactly what you'd call *haute cuisine*. So what else can you do? Well, there's no end to human ingenuity...

CAKE

• If you must cook directly in a fire (and it is rather *passé* these days) try caking your meat in a juicy coating of good thick mud – it'll make it a lot more succulent, and reduces the drying up and shrinkage that direct heat often causes. Don't forget to break off the mud before you eat it!

HOLE

• Slow cooking is always better – try wrapping your meat in a big leaf and cooking on embers rather than a roaring fire.

If you're feeling really sophisticated you can make an oven by digging a hole in the ground, filling the bottom with red-hot embers and covering up the top with a thick covering of leaves, twigs and straw. Be warned though, it can take several days to cook your food, so forward planning is called for.

PLUCK

• Another way to cook is by boiling – this means heating water until it bubbles, and then popping your food in. (Be sure to extract it with a small knife or stick. Do not, under any circumstances, pluck it from the water with your bare hands, no matter how hungry you are.)

If you're reading this before your tribe has invented cooking pots you'll have to boil the water in a big turtle shell or reptile skin. Some enterprising chefs in Central America have even gone to the trouble of hollowing out a large stone.

SHOOT

Readers in Asia may like to clean out a thick bamboo shoot and fill that with meat, veg and a little water. Keep the bamboo far enough away from the heat to stop it catching fire, and you'll have a delicious meal. *Bon appetit,* as we like to say in this part of the world.

Hunters! Deer make a tasty dish, but people are <u>so</u> soppy about them. Tell your family they're eating warthog, or they may never speak to you again.

IN STYLE

FOOD FACT HOT POT

HANDY HINTS
FOR HUNGRY READERS

- Readers in the chillier parts of the world will be interested to know that meat keeps fresh much longer if you bury it in the ground. This is particularly useful if you've killed something really big, and you can't carry it all back to your cave.

- Those of you who are still hunter-gatherers may like to try digging into the ground, rather than just picking fruit and vegetables from the trees and the top soil. Readers in Europe will be interested to know that several nutritious and (fairly) digestible vegetables, such as the turnip, onion and radish can be dug up with very little effort.

American readers will be able to find potatoes and yams.

All these vegetables can be spotted by their tell-tale shoots, and they all taste much nicer after you've boiled them for 20 minutes.

- Insects make an ideal snack! Yes, it's true! Dried locusts are 75% protein and 20% fat. (That only leaves 5% grisly bits too horrible to contemplate.) So, *courage, mes enfants,* next time you're out on a forage and hunger strikes, munch on a moth!

FISHY STORIES

Fish make a fabulous feast and they're cheap and wholesome!

They're not the brightest sparks in the world, and anyone wanting a pet to cuddle and adore would be ill-advised to keep one, but MAKE NO MISTAKE fish make a fabulous feast!

But how do you get hold of these silvery, slippery, succulent delicacies? FIND OUT with our infallible guide below.

BATTING

North American readers have seen Grizzly Bears do it by batting fish out of the water with their paws. Although we're quite a bit brighter than Grizzlies, for some reason we never got the hang of this.

Pierre says: *Buf! Worth a go if you're desperate.*

CLUBBING

You're no fool when you use a tool! Mind you, the splashing drives off any fish you haven't hit for miles around, and do watch out you don't club your own foot.

Pierre says: *Alors! It's a bit crude, but then this IS the Stone Age after all.*

TRAPPING

Gather up loads of sticks and laboriously lace them together to make a solid square barrier. Make several of these and then painstakingly arrange them in a V-shape reaching from the middle of the river to the bank, with a little gap at the pointy end of the V to let the fish in. Secure them to the river bed using boulders. When fish venture in, they're much easier to catch as they can't escape!

Pierre says: *Zut, mes amis! This sounds harder work than killing a mammoth.*

This man knows that fish bring style and sophistication to any table.

FISHING BOATS

If you're reading this before 8000BC, when we invent the oar, you'll have to wait a while, unless you're really foolhardy. With oars we'll have a more-than-likely chance of getting back alive when we venture out to sea in little reed rafts or dugout wooden canoes.

The best way to catch fish out at sea is with a big net. You can make one of these with twisted strands of hair or twine all roped together.

Pierre says: *Mon Dieu! Quite the most dangerous fishing technique available.*

Sharks, whirlpools, deadly currents and tides, blistering winds and huge, huge waves await. Still, it's quite pleasant when the sun's out, and you're in with a serious chance of catching a big load of fish.

FISH HOOK

Make a hook from a horn, using a flint tool. Attach a length of string made from wool or gut. Place worm on hook. Put in river with other end of string tied to big toe. Nod off to sleep. When toe feels a twitch, pull in line – you've scored!

Pierre says: *Formidable! This sounds too good to be true!*

NEXT WEEK: FAST FOOD AND HOW TO CATCH IT

Dazzy Dork's

WHAT'S HAPPENING COLUMN

SO WHO PUT THE BOMP IN THE BEAT?

Noted music profs reckon the first music happened when we discovered we could SING. Maybe we tried to imitate animal noises, maybe it was a nice hot day and we started to hum *Summertime and the living is easy* – who knows!

Then we started clapping our hands and banging sticks together, and discovered RHYTHM. Once we'd discovered that, the urge to shake our funky tail feathers and GET DOWN came upon us, and we started dancing.

Finally, we began to invent musical instruments. Maybe this started when a hunter noticed that his bow string went THWONGGGG when he fired an arrow, and he thought, "I could write a symphony with this!"

"You put your left leg in, and your left leg out..." If that's what it's all about, say dancers, we'll sit this one out.

DANCE FLOOR NEWS FLASH

Movers and shakers – we all like to stamp our feet when we're strutting our funky stuff, so why not beef up that beat with an anklet of shells from the beach?

If you live inland, save yourself a trip to the seaside by stringing together rows of bones or teeth to give your dance steps that added KER-CHINKKK!

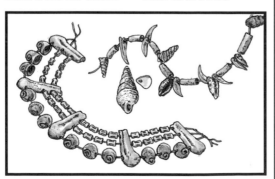

These sophisticated percussion instruments are operated by the ankle or wrist.

STONE-AGE TOP FIVE

1. Jailhouse Auroch **Elvis Zogley**
2. Where the tracks have no name **Ug2**
3. (I can't get no) huntin'-action **The Stones**
4. Eye of the (sabre-toothed) tiger **Bokk**
5. I'm a firestarter **Stigg and the Dumps**

INSTRUMENT NEWS

TOOT THAT FLUTE, ZOOT

So what's hot in the world of MUSICAL INSTRUMENTS?

next to your open mouth – you'll find it makes quite a difference to the volume (not to mention the state of your teeth.)

BUDUM BUDUM

Drummers! If you're still banging a stick on a tree, you've missed the boat maaaan! Get on the scene by stretching an animal skin over a clay pot or coconut half. You can play this with your fingers, or a stick. Alternatively, a mammoth skull makes a wonderful drum and gives a deeply satisfying K-DONK when you hit it with a heavy stick. And unlike a tree, you can take these kind of drums anywhere!

PLINK PLINK

Tight strings make all sorts of interesting sounds, but they're so QUIET. Try placing the string over the mouth of a pot as you twang it, or holding the string

TOOT TOOT

Which smart alec with nothing better to do discovered you could make musical notes by blowing into a bone? Gosh, that must have been an extremely long, wet Sunday afternoon! Well you CAN, and here's how.

• Take one medium sized bird bone.
• Hollow it out.
• Add a little tube to blow into at one end.
• Make four holes along the length of the bone.

You can make different whistling noises by covering up different holes.

Be sure to tell your musician pals that this is called a flute. We'll be seeing a lot more of this kind of instrument in the future!

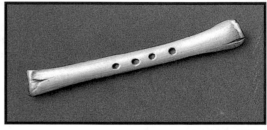

The flute with the tootiest toot this side of Toot House, Toot Street, Tootville!

DAZZY DORK'S NOTABLE NOTE OF THE DAY!

Hey kids! They say "music hath charms to soothe the savage beast". Personally, I'd rather face a tiger armed with a long spear than a bone flute, but, HEY, who can deny the STRANGE POWER of music!

GOOD HEALTH

THE STONE AGE WAY

with Robin Hukk, the Sentinel's medical correspondent

The column that keeps YOU up to the minute with the world of HEALTH and MEDICINE.

ILL-UMINATING!

Readers often ask where illnesses come from. Most of us in the medical profession believe that minor ailments, such as runny noses, or constipation, are just part of the great ebb and flow of human existence.

However, really big ailments, like being too poorly to stand up, or being covered in lurid boils, are due to supernatural causes. Perhaps the gods are angry with you, or a malevolent demon has cast a spell on you.

Either way, if you're <u>that</u> ill, something awesome thinks you've really blotted your copy book.

GOOD NEWS FOR SOME

Sentinel readers don't need me to tell you that it's a dangerous, unpleasant world out there. We get parched in the summer heat, and then we spend the winter shivering in our miserable tents and huts. We could get eaten by a pack of wolves one minute, or murdered by a gang of passing nomads the next.

THINGS

But don't despair, things are looking up. Thanks to recent improvements in diet, and more sophisticated weapons to protect us from predators, the average *Hom sap sap* man of 10,000 BC can now expect to live for a phenomenal 30 years!

DRAWS

There's not such good news for the ladies, however. Having drawn the biological short straw of child-bearing duties, most of you can still expect a visit from the grim reaper in your mid 20s. Still, chin up, at least you don't have to go mammoth hunting!

Healthy outdoor pursuits and a good diet all mean we're living longer.

TREATMENT CORNER

Two techniques to tell you about on the treatment front. The first is for minor ailments and the second is serious do-or-die stuff.

1. Upset stomach? Nagging headache? Festering cut? "Put on those gardening gloves," say tribes who have caught on to the fact that many plants contain healing substances. You can eat them directly, or boil them up in water, or make a paste to put on a wound, the variations are endless. The 64,000 pebble question is which plant for what ailment? Here at the *Sentinel* information is very sketchy, so we say "Have fun finding out!"

Take two of these, three times a day, with water.

2. Hold tight! Medical opinion has it that the gods make people ill by putting something bad into their body like a demon or a worm, or taking something out – like the patient's soul. Treatment for these ailments consists of either putting the soul back, or casting the intruder out. In such cases plant medicine can sometimes be effective, but more often than not, drastic methods are called for.

WHICH WITCH?

You may need to go to the expense of asking your local witchdoctor to perform a healing ceremony. (This will involve a lot of dancing and chanting, so be considerate and warn the people next door.)

WHOLE HOLE

Failing that, you could go for a trepanning. This involves having a hole drilled in your head. The advantages are that the demon or worm can then escape, or your soul can get back in. The disadvantages are extreme pain and likely death. Still, it's always worth a try if you're desperate!

THE BEGINNER'S GUIDE TO

BITING THE DUST

ANOTHER READER'S SERVICE

OUR FUNERAL CORRESPONDENT DAN DED REPORTS ON THE ULTIMATE SEND-OFF

Being buried is becoming increasingly fashionable among modern day hominids. In fact it's a sure sign that life is looking up! When you find you have time to think about what happens after you bite the dust, it means life isn't quite as nasty, brutish and short as it used to be.

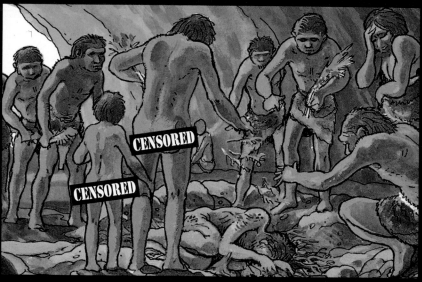

Funerals in Stone Age times are refreshingly informal, and stiff, black suits are definitely not required. It is essential, though, to bring flowers.

Testify!

Being the bright sparks we are, we've decided that we have a soul which lives on after death, and that dying is simply the moment when the soul leaves the body.

Whether you believe it goes to Heaven, the great Mammoth hunting ground in the sky, or simply lurks around your tomb or cave, depends on what idea your tribe has come up with.

Vultures

In the olden days, when we were *Homo habilis* and *Homo erectus*, experts think we were so busy finding food and avoiding being eaten we didn't make a fuss about dying at all.

If you dropped down dead, everybody else just left you there until you were eaten by a vulture. But these days we like to send our loved ones off in style, and here at the *Sentinel* we've been nosing around to see how it's done.

Neanderthal style

40,000 BC
Neanderthals were the first hominids to bury their dead, and they certainly went extinct

with a flourish!
• They dug a hole in the floor of a cave and laid the body on pine branches in a sleeping position, with its head resting on a stone pillow.
• Then they covered the body with flowers, and added some tools and a little food in case they'd be needed in the afterlife. Then they covered everything up with a nice snug layer of soil.*

Flowers will brighten up any funeral, and cost virtually nothing!

Homo Sapiens style

27,000 BC onwards
As you'd expect, *Hom Sap* does things with a bit more sophistication.
• If you're pretty important then you're buried in some really fancy clothing – furs, hats embroidered with seashells, tunics with fox-tooth decoration, you know the sort of stuff.
• In Russia they like to bury important people with THOUSANDS of elaborately carved little

mammoth-ivory beads arranged in rows around the body.
• In France and Czechoslovakia they cover the bodies with red clay. (We think this represents blood and life.) In parts of France they also wrap the dead tightly in cloth to prevent the spirit re-entering the body and making a nuisance of itself. (Spoil-sports! Here at the *Sentinel*, we think this

Funerals can be fun, so be prepared to let your hair down!

might make for an exciting evening's enter-tainment. After all, it'll be a while yet before anyone gets around to inventing television.)

Stones

And if you're reading this after 4,500 BC you may be interested to know that in Europe they're burying their dead in really impressive megaliths.

These are artificial caves made up of massive, heavy stones. They make an ideal shelter for a dead body, or depending on their size, a whole bunch of dead bodies.

So there, being dead doesn't have to mean being lonely. Now there's a comforting thought!

Au naturel

Finally, over in North America, *Hom Sap* is doing things the simple way. They don't bother with anything elaborate, and rightly so. What could be easier than your so-called "Sky Burial"?

What you do is put your deceased in a high spot – up on a mountain, the top of a tree – and leave them to the weather and any passing animal who feels like a nibble.

When there's just a pile of bones left, you take these away and bury them. Ahhh, we do like to be different, don't we!?!

*Experts now disagree about the intention of Neanderthal burials. See page 10 for details.

SE TINEL SUPER ATURAL SPECIAL

STAGMAN!

WILL KURRR MEETS A MAN WITH ANTLERS ON HIS HEAD

A secret camera captures Rik Vog's witchdoctor rituals for the *SENTINEL*. Hey Rik, don't put a spell on us!

Let's face it. There's got to be more to existence than "Kill mammoths, then die". What's life all about? Do supernatural beings control our lives? Can we persuade the gods to look after US, rather than that tribe in the next valley who never invites us to their parties?

In this special feature, *Sentinel* religion correspondent Will Kurrr interviews a man who thinks he has the answers. It's Witchdoctor Rick Vog, of Les Trois Frères, France.

Will Kurrr: So Rik, what's with the antlers and everything?

Rick Vog: Hi, Will. This is my witchdoctor outfit. I wear it to frighten little children! Ha ha ha, just kidding. Actually, the antlers and stag mask are part of my priestly garments, along with a generous daubing of body paint.

I get dressed up like this at religious ceremonies, where all the men in our tribe gather together in a deep dark cave. I lead them through sacred rituals to ensure that the stags and deer that we hunt will
continue to live in our part of the world, and we'll never go hungry.

WK: So what do you do exactly?

RV: BIG SECRET. If I told you in detail other tribes would copy us, and they'd lure our animals away. I can tell you we do a lot of dancing, and chanting, and we hand around magical objects carved out of antler and bone, and we sacrifice some animals too.

WK: So what's the point of that?

RV: It's MAGIC! You have to perform your rituals exactly right of course. Mix up your chants, or hand around the sacred object the wrong way, and it doesn't work! I've been doing this for five years, and our tribe has never gone hungry once.

WK: So how does it work?

RV: There are lots of spirits floating around
out there. They live in the most beautiful parts of the land, like waterfalls or the forest.

There are spirits in the air, and water, and earth, and fire. Some are good, some are evil. The whole point of these rituals is to keep the friendly spirits sweet with sacrifices and worship, so they'll keep you in food and good weather. If you neglect them, they leave you to the mercy of bad spirits, and that means your tribe starves because there's nothing to hunt, and everyone suffers from diseases.

WK: It sounds like a pretty important job!

RV: Too right. You can't leave anything to chance these days. We need to put a huge amount of time and effort into these ceremonies to keep us fed and healthy.

Besides which, dressing up like this is much more fun than hunting mammoths, or picking berries, but don't tell anyone in my tribe I told you!

THE SENTINEL — IT'S SPOOKILY GOOD!

A SENTINEL QUIZ FOR THE WHOLE FAMILY TO ENJOY!!!

NAME THAT TOOL!

QUESTIONABLE QUESTIONS FOR THE MECHANICALLY MINDED

ANSWERS

❶ b) It's a tray made out of tree bark. You can collect berries in this.

❷ b) It's a saw. It's just right for cutting meat and grass.

❸ a) It's for straightening spears. You place your slightly bent wooden pole in it, and bend it 'til it's straight. Piece of cake!

❹ a) It's a chisel all right. You can shape antler, bone and wood with the sharp end of that.

❺ c) They <u>were</u> both wrong, it is a drill! You can make little holes in hide, fur, ivory, wood, in fact anything you like, with this tool.

❻ c). No, I'm just kidding, it's really b). You can make one of these with a sliver of ivory and tools 4 and 5.

❼ a) Of course it's a harpoon.

❽ a) Although the *Sentinel* in no way approves or condones any acts of gratuitous violence, we have to agree with a) that this item is most definitely a dugout canoe.

❾ b) Ha ha. Fooled you. It IS just a piece of rock. Incidentally, a lava hammerstone is what you use when you want to hit and shape another piece of stone.

We all know that tools have enabled us to **RULE THE WORLD**, and anyone worth a stuffed field mouse knows what an axe or a spear looks like. But what about THESE odd looking things? Guess what they are, as we ask "What on Earth is THAT?"

❶
a) A bangle?
b) A tray?
c) An early attempt at wallpaper?

❷
a) er.. Is it a pastry shaper?
b) It's a saw.
c) Scrubbing brush?

❸
a) Hang on, I know this. It's for straightening spears, isn't it?
b) Is it some kind of stone pillow?
c) It's a chopstick rest.

❹
a) That's got to be a chisel.
b) No. It's a saxophone mouthpiece. I know. My brother plays one.
c) It's a fractional distillation chamber.

❺
a) Now that's a toothpick.
b) No, it's a spade.
c) You're both wrong. It's a drill.

❻
a) It's a microscope.
b) No, hang on, it's a needle!
c) You're both wrong again. It's a transmission gear connecting rod, and I know that for a FACT.

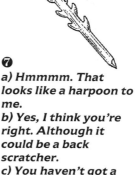

❼
a) Hmmmm. That looks like a harpoon to me.
b) Yes, I think you're right. Although it could be a back scratcher.
c) You haven't got a clue. It's OBVIOUS that it's a hat stand.

❽
a) It's a dugout canoe.
b) Naaaah, it's a toothbrush holder.
c) You're both complete cretins. Any fool can see that it's some sort of wheelbarrow.
a) I don't like your manner. Take that, punk! (CLUNK, THONK, BOP BOP BOP.)
c) Aaaaaaaaagh.

❾
a) Now that's got to be a lava hammerstone.
b) Come off it, it's just a piece of rock, anyone can see that.

ILLUSTRATION CREDITS

Guy Smith

and Bob Hersey, Rob McCaig, Karen Tomlins and Gerald Wood.

PHOTO CREDITS

AKG Photo, London (pages 11, 12, 23); Ancient Art and Architecture Collection, London (page 20); Robert Harding Photo Library/Rainbird, London (page 9).